**TS-110
Keeping
and
Breeding
PARROTS**

Photographers: Toni Angermayer, Dr. Herbert R. Axelrod, Cliff Bickford, Th. Brosset, Chelman and Petrulla, Wolfgang de Grahl, G. Ebben, Isabelle Francais, Michael Gilroy, Fred Harris, Ralph Kaehler, S. Kates, Harry V. Lacey, Midori Shobo, Ron and Val Moat, A.J. Mobbs, Irene and Michael Morcombe, P. Munchenberg, K.T. Nemuras, Klaus Paysan, H. Pinter, Fritz Prenzel, H. Reinhard, L. Robinson, San Diego Zoo, Louise Van Der Meid, Vogelpark Walsrode.

Artists: J. Gould, Eric Peake, R.A. Vowles.

Title page: Scaly-headed Parrot, one of the many fascinating members of the parrot family.

Originally published in German by Albrecht Philler Verlag under the title *Die Papageien*. First edition ©1971 by Albrecht Philler Verlag.

A considerable amount of additional new material has been added to the literal German-English translation, including but not limited to additional photographs. Copyright is also claimed for this new material.

Distributed in the UNITED STATES by T.F.H. Publications, Inc., One T.F.H. Plaza, Neptune City, NJ 07753; in CANADA to the Pet Trade by H & L Pet Supplies Inc., 27 Kingston Crescent, Kitchener, Ontario N2B 2T6; Rolf C. Hagen Ltd., 3225 Sartelon Street, Montreal 382 Quebec; in CANADA to the Book Trade by Macmillan of Canada (A Division of Canada Publishing Corporation), 164 Commander Boulevard, Agincourt, Ontario M1S 3C7; in ENGLAND by T.F.H. Publications Limited, Cliveden House/Priors Way/Bray, Maidenhead, Berkshire SL6 2HP, England; in AUSTRALIA AND THE SOUTH PACIFIC by T.F.H. (Australia) Pty. Ltd., Box 149, Brookvale 2100 N.S.W., Australia; in NEW ZEALAND by Ross Haines & Son, Ltd., 82 D Elizabeth Knox Place, Panmure, Auckland, New Zealand; in the PHILIPPINES by Bio-Research, 5 Lippay Street, San Lorenzo Village, Makati Rizal; in SOUTH AFRICA by Multipet Pty. Ltd., Box 235, New Germany, South Africa 3620. Published by T.F.H. Publications, Inc. Manufactured in the United States of America by T.F.H. Publications, Inc.

Keeping and Breeding
PARROTS
Carl Aschenborn

Contents

Opposite: A pair of Green-winged Macaws engaged in mutual preening.

A Senegal Parrot, one of many African parrots.

Introduction

Within the system of birds, parrots form an order in their own right—Psittaformes—here divided into 12 families (as based on the works on parrot taxonomy by Verheyen von Boetticher, Brereton and Immelmann, Brereton, Holyoak, and Smith). Some authors recognize only a single family with a varying number of subfamilies; others in turn distribute the parrots over four or six families. These strongly divergent interpretations result from the fact that, while the basic structure of the body is very much the same in all parrots, there is a great diversity as far as the details are concerned. Sibley (1972), when carrying out his protein analyses, also discovered considerable variations between the individual groups. A similar multiplicity of forms, colors, and, indeed, of sizes is not shown by many groups of birds.

The typical characteristic of parrots is the strong beak, which is similar in shape to that of a bird of prey. The parrot's beak is higher, however, as well as being shorter and more strongly curved than that of a bird of prey. But like the latter's, it has a soft waxlike structure, known as "cere," at the base of its upper part which encloses the circular nostril. In most species, the upper mandible, which is curved like a hook, has several horizontal grooves. The function of these is dual: they make it easier for the bird to hold on to seeds, and they enable it to sharpen the anterior edge of the lower mandible. The tongue is thick and fleshy and in some species—the Lories— is covered in fibrous papillae, like a "brush," which facilitate the lapping of nectar, fruit and tree juices. Since the parrot's beak is also intended for grasping and climbing, the upper mandible is extraordinarily mobile.

Further typical characteristics of parrots are the legs, the short, thick tarsus, and the four toes of the fleshy foot, of which, as in the woodpeckers, the first and fourth point backward and the second and third point forward, thus forming a

particularly effective prehensile organ.

Except in Europe, parrots are found as native to every continent, i.e., in the warmer regions. The majority of them live in forests, but there are also numerous species that favor the steppes; a small minority are birds of high mountains which even occur above the tree-line. Parrots usually lead a gregarious life. Some of them actually breed in colonies, and all of them are strictly monogamous. They feed predominantly on vegetable matter, i.e., all kinds of seeds, fruits, buds, roots, tubers. A few live on honey, fruit and tree juices. Some also take insects, worms, etc. Their water requirements are minimal, as a rule. With the exception of one species which builds free-standing nests (the Quaker or Monk Parakeet) and a few other species that breed on the open ground (Ground Parrots), they nest inside hollows in trees, rocks, or the soil. The eggs of all parrots are white.

Parrots have a loud voice, often a shrieking one. Those of the large species utter deafening screams. On the other hand, many a small species can produce fairly pleasant sounds, and the subdued twittering of some is quite appealing. The great talent for "talking," notably where the larger species are concerned, is well-known—i.e., that they are able to mimic or repeat words of human speech—as is also their ability to whistle tunes. There are real artists among them which acquire a large vocabulary and are able to "speak" whole sentences. They are totally unable to comprehend the *meaning* of these, however, and I would like to stress this particularly here—even if they seem to be "on cue" when they "say" them and thus give the impression that the words make sense to them. They possess an excellent capacity for observation and association which enables them

to find the "right" word for specific situations. But discernment, though, and conscious reasoning are absent. The mental endowment of a bird is not sufficient for that. Rather, their "speech" is the product of conditioning or associating, i.e., the simplest mental activity and one for which rational or logical thinking are not required. This association

A striking Scarlet Macaw. In the wild, Macaws often travel and live in large, colorful flocks.

"Parrots usually lead a gregarious life. Some of them actually breed in colonies, and all of them are strictly monogamous."

A pair of Splendid Parakeets. These birds are often called Scarlet-chested Parrots. This species is found on the continent of Australia.

A Scaly-breasted Lorikeet. This bird makes a lively pet, but it is said to be potentially dangerous to smaller birds.

Hoopoe: an Old World, nonpasserine bird (family Upupidae) that has a slender, decurved bill.

consists of the purely external linking of two events in such a way that if one of them occurs, the other is automatically experienced at the same time. An example may serve to make this clear. What follows was related by the well-known ornithologist from Berlin, D. Fr. von Lucanus, who was particularly interested in the inner life of parrots. Among the many pet birds he kept in his home was a very tame hoopoe that had been given the name "Hoopy." This word was soon picked up and applied to the hoopoe by a Grey Parrot. The hoopoe died after a few months; the word "Hoopy" was not said in the household anymore, not by the Grey Parrot, either—in fact, the latter seemed to have lost it from its vocabulary. Two years later von Lucanus received another hoopoe. As soon as the parrot clapped eyes on it, it shouted, "Hoopy." So it had not forgotten the word "Hoopy" in those two years and had immediately recognized another hoopoe when it saw one—a very considerable achievement which shows what excellent memories Grey Parrots have!

Parrots were favored as pets in antiquity, and in those ancient times people kept "talking" animals which fetched a high price. In Ancient Rome, for instance, the price of a "talking" psittacine bird often exceeded the value of a slave. In Germany, parrots were first seen at the time of the Crusades. It was not until America had been discovered, however, that parrot-keeping became so tremendously popular in Europe, due to the increasing importation of more and more new species from an area where, even today, the natives still keep free-flying tame parrots as pets and are exceptionally skilled at taming these animals quickly and thoroughly.

There has also been a constant supply of newly discovered species from other parts of the globe. I am thinking particularly of the various agapornids from Africa, which first appeared on the market in the '20s and held their ground until the accursed psittacosis triggered the ban on parrot imports in 1934 and imposed substantial restrictions on the hobby. Neither psittacosis nor the legal measures it prompted have been able to detract from the popularity of parrots, however.

Psittacosis: an infectious disease of birds which is transmissible to man and to poultry, often called parrot fever.

A trio of Sun Conures enjoying some sunshine in their outdoor aviary.

Cage, Birdroom, and Aviary

Crop: an enlarged pouch in the gullet in which food is ground, usually with the aid of ingested sand or gravel.

Generally speaking, the specifications for parrot cages are different from those for cages that accommodate other species of birds. For one thing, they must be made completely of metal because of the gnawing instinct and the strong beaks of many species of parrots. Only in exceptional circumstances can cages with wooden frames—hardwood, such as normally employed for seed eaters—be used. Further, it must be borne in mind that many species—especially the larger ones, of course—are able to pry apart the standard metal bars with their beaks and even to bite through ordinary small wire mesh. It goes without saying that wooden pull-out trays are totally unsuitable,

A Grey Parrot. Grey Parrots are especially renowned for their speaking ability and their wonderful memories.

too, and that food and water containers must be strong. It is important, also, that the doors of the cages close securely so that these agile animals cannot open them with their beaks.

As can be seen, there is quite a lot that needs to be taken into consideration when it comes to buying a parrot cage. The length of such a cage should be a minimum of 1 m for the smallest species and not less than 1.5 m for the larger ones. As permanent accommodation this is too cramped, however, and it is appropriate only where the bird can be granted free flight inside the room every day. Cages made of brass wire should be rejected, even if, as is often the case nowadays, they have been coated with varnish to prevent the formation of verdigris. It is obviously very easy for the parrot to remove all traces of the varnish within the shortest possible time.

Single cages for large parrots are generally fitted with a wide-meshed wire grid at some small distance from the bottom, which prevents the bird from gaining access to the floor of the cage and getting dirty there. What is overlooked here, however, is that this prevents the ingestion of sand and gravel, which all seed eaters need for grinding the seeds inside the crop. In these cases, the two grinding agents should be supplied in a special dish. Chief-Keeper Roelvinck of the Cologne Zoo, with years of experience behind him, blames the excessive growth of beaks and claws on this type of grid, since the absence of sand deprives the birds of an essential prerequisite

An Eastern Rosella. This bird is difficult to find, as it has been excessively hybridized with other species of Rosellas.

A pair of Moustached Parakeets, beautiful birds which make good pets once they get past the screaming stage.

"The ideal form of housing. . .is a birdroom or, better still, an outdoor aviary. Here, it is not only easier to achieve good breeding results but the animals also come into their own much more and are able to behave more naturally."

for wear and tear to their beaks and claws. He considers it necessary not only that the bottom of the cage be covered with sand but that a stone—about the size of a pigeon's egg—be put into the cage in addition, enabling the bird to sharpen its beak.

Perches, twigs and branches with bark on them also should be provided. These will need to be replaced every so often since they frequently get gnawed by the parrots. Be sure the twigs are taken from trees that have not been sprayed with chemicals of any kind or exposed to car exhaust fumes.

Cages intended to accommodate several parrots must be very spacious. In all cases where several pairs of the same or of different species of parrots are to be kept together, extreme caution is a necessity, as the birds are often cantankerous and ill-natured, even outside the breeding season. The

bigger the cage, the less is the danger of squabbles since it is easier for the animals to keep out of each other's way.

The ideal form of housing, of course, is a birdroom or, better still, an outdoor aviary. Here, it is not only easier to achieve good breeding results but the animals also come into their own much more and are able to behave more naturally.

Any room that gets sunshine at some time or other is suitable as a birdroom. It must be possible to heat this room, however, even if many species tolerate temperate climate fairly well, and many can actually be kept out-of-doors all year 'round without any qualms. Heaters, fires, radiators, or even heat lamps, should be fenced off at some distance by means of wire mesh so that the birds, which like to get close to sources of heat, do not burn their feet. The window opening should also be covered with wire mesh in such a way that the window is easy to open and shut. If circumstances permit, a small projecting structure should be built outside in front of the window. This should have a firm floor and be fitted with wire mesh all round. Such a "balcony" enables the animals not only to sunbathe but also to expose themselves to the rain, which some parrots particularly enjoy since they do not bathe.

That plants are out of place in a birdroom stocked with parrots makes sense, since they would not stand up to those beaks for very long. Climbing trees should, however, be put up, as well as branches and twigs. All of these must be fitted in such a way that the animals still have ample flying space. Since many species like to spend the night inside boxes, a few nestboxes should always be present outside the breeding season, too. It must be borne in mind that some species like boxes that hang in a bright spot, whereas others prefer the reverse. There should not be any wallpaper in a birdroom; any already present must be removed and the walls white-washed. The floor must be carefully sealed and sprinkled with sand. Finally, the birdroom should be fitted with a lamp so that the birds can be given more time to feed during the winter months. The fancier may decide to install a time switch so that the light goes on and off automatically and perhaps gradually as well.

The fancier who has a garden can build his own aviary here, i.e., an outdoor flight. The size obviously depends on how much space is available, and the same applies where the construction of a special birdhouse is concerned. The latter, with an aviary attached to it or even several aviaries, constitutes the best form of accommodation for the birds.

There are several important points I would like to mention. A concrete or brick foundation serves as protection against rats and mice. A brick or concrete enclosure with its base 50 cm below ground would constitute a fairly effective alternative, however. The side walls of the aviary (consisting of fine wire mesh) would go on top of this. For the roof, wire mesh can be used, although roughly half the roof should consist of solid material to afford protection against rain, snow, and the sun. It is also important that there is a corner which is sheltered from the wind. This can be improvised with glass panes (wire

Yellow-naped Amazon Parrot. No matter what species of parrot you plan to keep, the cage must never be too small.

Open-air flight: the portion of the aviary that has at least one wall that is not solid, usually constructed of wire mesh over support posts.

glass), plastic, or wood. An indoor shelter with some form of heating is vital, too. Only a few species can be kept in an open-air flight during the winter months, and this ought to have at least one solid wall, but even these species prefer an indoor shelter during severe weather. A double door is essential. It alone makes it impossible for the inmates to escape when someone enters the aviary.

The importance of keeping cats at bay needs to be given special emphasis. Marauding cats can drive an aviary owner to despair. Many aviary birds have been maimed or killed by cats! There are, of course, entirely effective remedies that provide a radical cure in persistent cases. However, for a variety of reasons these are out of place here or cannot be mentioned. A fairly good method of protecting the aviary is to put up a double layer of wire all around it, with a distance of about five to ten centimeters between the two layers. The roof should be protected in the same way. This measure is guaranteed to prevent the

A pair of White-eared Conures. White-eared Conures are fairly active birds, and they have been bred in captivity.

birds from being attacked through the wire, and not only provides protection against cats and other furry predators but also against birds of prey such as the sparrow hawk and the barn owl.

Planting the parrot aviary is hardly feasible where larger species are involved—or, to be more precise, it is ill advised—since the inmates' beaks would quickly and utterly destroy the vegetation. Where smaller species are concerned, or species with a less severe gnawing urge, one can try one's luck with all sorts of shrubs or small trees. Most suitable above all, in such cases, are conifers. But even here it will almost certainly prove necessary to replace the plants every so often. One way to enhance the external appearance of the aviary is to train climbing roses, clematis, and other creepers and climbers up the corner posts and perhaps to have a narrow herbaceous border or a strip of grass all around the aviary. This is a matter of personal taste, however.

In this connection it should be pointed out that parrots in general have rather loud voices (some of them positively shriek) and not only get on the owner's nerves but above all can become a nuisance to the neighbors. It is prudent, therefore, before building a garden aviary, to question whether the members of the parrot family for which it is intended can, in fact, be tolerated by the neighbors. Otherwise one will be causing oneself a lot of trouble, and a great deal of work will have been for nothing.

THE PARROT STAND

Individual tame parrots—above all the big Macaws, the Amazons and Cockatoos—may be kept on a special stand during the day and be put in the cage only over night. They can, however, also be left on the parrot stand the whole time. The advantage

A pair of Orange-bellied Fig Parrots, a male and a female. The male is the upper, more brightly colored bird.

"Parrot stands come in many different designs. . . .they can be purchased at one of the bigger pet shops. These generally have a variety of them in stock, among them some fairly elegant models."

for the bird is greater freedom of movement than it would have in the cage and for the keeper to get an unimpeded view of his pet.

Parrot stands come in many different designs. Anyone with even a slight experience in using tools can easily make one. Virtually every bird fancier will have made something or other at some point! Alternatively, they can be purchased at one of the bigger pet shops. These generally have a variety of them in stock, among them some fairly elegant models. A high perch, and a movable one at that, more closely mimics natural conditions and, consequently, the bird prefers it to a low perch and an immovable rod.

The upper bird is a Vernal Hanging Parrot while the lower is a Blue-crowned Hanging Parrot. These birds are named for their ability to sleep hanging upside-down.

A pair of Hyacinth Macaws, members of the largest parrot species in the world. Larger parrots need ample freedom of movement; once tame, they can be kept on special parrot stands or on a climbing tree.

For the keeper's benefit, the bird's perch should be at eye level. The food vessels must be firmly attached so that the bird cannot knock them off or upset them. It is also important to position them where their contents will not be fouled.

Finally, the climbing tree must not be forgotten. This is a thickish branch with plenty of shoots; in my opinion it is more pleasing to look at and offers more entertainment to the bird than a stand with completely straight perching rods. Whether a parrot has to be tethered to the stand (not exactly a commendable form of keeping) or whether it can be given complete liberty depends chiefly on how tame it is and how it copes with free flight. If the bird constantly leaves its stand and goes too far afield, tethering it will be unavoidable. The chain used for this purpose should have a length of about 25 to 30 cm, be sufficiently strong, and consist of smooth links (no sharp edges). It should be fastened to the stand by means of a ring in such a way that it moves to and fro without any difficulty. To prevent the chain from getting into a tangle when the bird climbs about, a shackle should be inserted on the first link of the chain, behind the foot ring. Tethering the bird to the climbing tree is not possible since the chain would inevitably become entangled during the bird's climbing activities.

A pair of Rainbow Lories. Lories need especially spacious aviaries since they are such agile fliers.

Climbing tree: a thick branch with several shoots which enable the bird to perch or climb at its leisure, usually much more attractive and certainly more natural than straight perches.

Nutrition and Feeding

A correct diet is absolutely essential for the successful keeping of pet birds. Everything depends primarily on nutrition: the well-being and health of the birds in one's care, whether breeding attempts have a satisfactory outcome, whether the young birds thrive. What is particularly important is that the food be in good condition. Where seeds are concerned, this means they need to be fresh. They must be intact and free from dust, and there must be no musty odor. They should be purchased at a special pet shop or from a feed supplier. The main constituents of parrot food, excluding the food for brush-tongued parrots, are high carbohydrate seeds such as millet, canary seed, oats, and a variety of grass seeds. For the larger species, maize and sunflower seeds should be added to this list. The latter can also be given to the smaller species, although in this case as a dietary supplement. Hemp is given, too, but, like the sunflower seeds, it should be fed in moderation, especially where smaller species are concerned, since these are oily seeds and therefore fattening. The bigger species also appreciate nuts, i.e., all the different varieties: walnuts, hazelnuts, peanuts, as well as pinenuts. Millet, canary seed, and oats should always be given in a soaked and germinated condition as well.

The germ of the seed contains not only vitamins A, B, D, and E but also enzymes, which are as important as vitamins and growth substances, trace elements, minerals, etc. In other words, it contains all the nutrients the body needs. So, depending on requirements, a number of shallow dishes are put out, filled with a not too deep layer of seeds, and then just enough water is poured over to just cover the seeds. The containers are covered

"A correct diet is absolutely essential for the successful keeping of pet birds. Everything depends primarily upon nutrition: the well-being of the birds in one's care, whether breeding attempts have a satisfactory outcome, whether the young birds thrive."

with a pane of glass and put in a warm place. Twenty-four to 36 hours later, the seeds will have been soaked sufficiently to be ready for feeding. If the seeds are still wet, they should be dried slightly on blotting paper. Any seeds that have grown moldy are unfit for consumption and must be destroyed. To obtain fresh greenfood, shallow flower bowls, boxes, or pots are filled with potting compost, plenty of seeds are put in, very close together, and then these containers, too, are covered with panes of glass and put into a warm spot. After three or four days, the seedlings will

be sufficiently long to be suitable as food. If possible, these bowls or pots should be put inside the cage at this stage to allow the birds to snack on them. This method of leaving seeds to sprout is especially appropriate in the winter when natural supplies of greenfood are not readily available.

Greenfood is absolutely essential if the birds are to remain healthy. Suitable plants to collect are chickweed, lettuce, spinach, dandelion, groundsel. All greenfood must be fresh, otherwise it is liable to cause intestinal disorders. In view of the ever-increasing use of chemical insecticides in recent years,

Greenfood: sprouted seed or various plants and vegetables which make wonderful supplements to the diet of pet parrots, a necessity for some species.

Normal and lutino Cockatiels and a Yellow-crowned Amazon getting ready to eat.

Yellow phase Peach-faced Lovebirds. Be sure to provide ample food for each bird you keep.

Cuttlebone: the internal dorsal shell of the cuttlefish, an important source of calcium for cage birds.

it is important to not collect plants where the fields or their edges have been sprayed. Food plants should, therefore, be collected only from scree slopes or other localities which one can safely assume have not been treated. In fact, your best bet is to purchase all food from your pet shop.

Berries and other fruits are a necessity for many parrots. Suitable is anything that happens to be in season, including dates, figs, raisins, and bananas. Carrots should not be absent from the diet, either.

In addition to seeds, the birds should be offered animal food, i.e., a soft-food mix such as can be obtained from pet shops. This is particularly important during the breeding season. Instead of a soft-food mix, alternatives can be ant pupae (fresh or dried), hard-boiled egg, or bread with a high egg content. Stale rolls, white bread, or rusks, soaked in milk, constitute a popular supplementary food. Finally, calcium must not be absent from the diet—crushed egg-shells or snail-shells, cuttlebone (the internal

Male Grand Eclectus Parrot. A good diet will go a long way toward keeping your parrot's plumage in good condition.

A Turquoise Parrot. Fresh branches are a treat for parrots; however, one must be sure that such branches have never been treated with chemicals. Pet shops often sell safe tree branches for parrot cages.

dorsal shell of the cuttlefish, *Ossa sepia)*, or a commercial calcium preparation.

To conclude the section on food, I would like to stress the importance of offering one's feathered charges as wide and varied a diet as possible. It must be pointed out here that the constant administering of vitamin preparations (from ignorance, usually at too high a dosage as well) can cause considerable damage to health. Only during the colder period, when there is relatively little sunshine, is there any good reason for enriching the food with things like cod-liver oil or a multi-vitamin preparation. And one other thing: the big parrots especially are often given food intended for human consumption. There is nothing wrong with that in principle, provided the food agrees with them. Under no circumstances, however, must they receive very salty or otherwise highly spiced foods.

As already mentioned, the parrots are characterized by having a more or less pronounced urge to gnaw. It is, therefore, necessary to supply them with fresh twigs which enable them to exercise the beak in this way. The thickness of the twigs depends on the species of parrot. Suitable above all are twigs from fruit trees, but also those from elderberry, willow, hazelnut, lime, or pine trees (for instance), all of which the birds chew up or strip. If birds with a strong gnawing instinct are not given the appropriate outlet, they invariably attack not only the perches but also destroy absolutely everything else that is made of wood—the nestboxes, for example.

Food dishes for parrots must be strong enough to withstand the beaks. For larger flights with several occupants, an automatic food dispenser is recommended. This saves the keeper a lot of trouble. Such feeders are commercially available; automatic water dispensers are also available at pet shops.

For bathing, any glass, china, or earthenware bowl is suitable. A flowerpot saucer, for instance, would do very well. Parrots which are less inclined to bathe, and above all the larger species, should be sprayed with a fine flower mister every so often.

". . . parrots are characterized by having a more or less pronounced urge to gnaw. It is, therefore, necessary to supply them with fresh twigs which enable them to exercise the beak in this way."

Breeding

Thoroughbred: a purebred bird that is a true representative of its species—not a hybrid or mixed breed.

Many species of parrots have been successfully bred in captivity, and especially during the last few years, i.e., since the animals have increasingly been kept in outdoor aviaries, notable successes have been achieved with regard to propagating species in captivity for the very first time. This does not mean, however, that parrots, the smaller species in particular, cannot be bred in the cage (which of course must be as spacious as possible). The bigger the cage, and the greater the freedom of movement for its inmates, the more likely is breeding to be successful.

Matching a breeding pair can sometimes be difficult. Quite apart from the fact that a female of the relevant species invariably may not be found on the market, it can happen that the two partners do not harmonize, that they take no notice of each other and are quite obviously incompatible. If this is the case the only thing to do is to replace one or other of the partners with a new bird. It is sensible, when matching a pair, to select young birds whose plumage has perhaps only just assumed the adult coloration. What is essential, however, is that both animals be healthy and in perfect condition.

Also important when matching breeding pairs is to make sure they are thoroughbreds so that the species continues to be preserved in a purebred state. Much sinning goes on in that respect, unfortunately,

Yellow-collared Macaws (outside the nest) and Rose-ringed Parakeets (inside the nest). One of the most fascinating aspects of breeding is watching the young birds gradually develop their adult plumage.

A male lutino
Budgerigar.
As a species
becomes more
common in
captivity, it is
often bred in
different color
phases.

Yellow-collared Macaws, Lesser Sulfur-crested Cockatoos, and a Blue-headed/White-capped Parrot hybrid.

Incubation: the act of keeping the clutch of eggs warm by sitting on them, performed by one or more of the parent birds.

and as a result of this it is difficult nowadays, and sometimes well-nigh impossible where some groups are concerned (for instance the Australian broadtails or the African lovebirds, the agapornids), to get truly purebred individuals with perfect colors.

Since most parrots breed in hollows, nestboxes must be provided, the dimensions of which have to be adapted to the bird's size. Suitable are boxes made of wooden boards (and their construction may be upright or broad) as well as natural tree trunks with the bark still on them. All of these are available on the market in a tremendous variety of sizes. Generally speaking, the nestboxes are fitted in such a way that the birds are still able to perch on top of them, but not immediately below the ceiling. A small minority of species prefer their boxes to be located on the aviary floor. The nesting-hollow inside the box is covered with a litter of leaf-

mold and sawdust which should be 2 to 3 cm deep.

Special care is indicated once the animals are incubating. Some species are extraordinarily sensitive even to the slightest disturbance; they desert eggs and young, and then all the trouble the keeper has been taking up to that point will have been in vain. It is essential, therefore, to contain one's curiosity and not to check as to whether there are any eggs lying in the nest or whether any young have hatched. I am convinced that a vast proportion of failures are directly related to the constant checking up on the incubating or feeding adult birds. I see no plausible reason for constantly disturbing the birds by opening the nestboxes, etc. This does not mean, of course, that the keeper should refrain from checking up if there is reason to suspect that something has gone wrong—for instance, if the young, normally very loud, cannot be heard for any length of time or if the adult birds appear to have stopped feeding their offspring. But, under normal circumstances, the best advice would be to intrude as little as possible.

If young are being raised, a special food needs to be given. This raising-food should not, however, suddenly appear after the young have hatched, but must be offered right from the beginning of the breeding season, so that the adult birds can gradually adapt to it and the keeper can find out which food they accept and which they reject. Then the correct raising-food can be provided when the time comes.

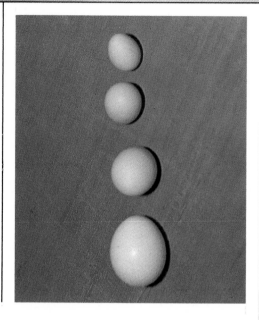

A comparison of various parrot eggs: Cockatoo (the largest), Grey Parrot, Cockatiel, and Budgerigar.

If you plan to breed your parrots, a proper nestbox is usually necessary.

Keeping and Maintenance

"Correct keeping and maintenance do not consist merely of providing the right diet and housing. What is important above all is that the keeper be conscientious with regard to cleanliness, both of the bird and its accommodation."

Correct keeping and maintenance do not consist merely of providing the right diet and housing. What is important above all is that the keeper be conscientious with regard to cleanliness, both of the bird and its accommodation. The bird keeper should take note of that, too. This means helping one's pet to keep scrupulously clean by providing fresh bathwater every day, or spraying the animal with water at least once a week, while at the same time keeping the cages and flights clean as well as everything inside them, such as food and water bowls, baths, perches, roosting and nestboxes, and making sure the floor covering is kept clean. It is vital, too, to be on the lookout for parasites, by which is meant the notorious red bird-mite. An effective control of this scourge of birds is no longer all that difficult today, thanks to a number of good insecticides, particularly the so-called contact insecticides, that have been evolved by the chemical industry. When necessary, the bird fancier should go to a pet shop or a veterinarian for advice.

In addition to the plumage, the feet also require special attention so that inflammations are prevented. Crucial, in this respect, is that the perches be kept clean. In some species of parrots, the horny tissue of the beak has a tendency to proliferate either laterally or anteriorly. In such cases, the beak needs to be trimmed carefully to resume its natural shape. This must be done without causing it to bleed. By providing the bird with fresh twigs, it has the opportunity to nibble and gnaw and so encourage the natural wear and tear of the beak.

In some cases the twigs also turn out to be a remedy for feather-picking, which occurs when birds pluck out their own feathers, often due to boredom. Such individuals should also be given plenty of opportunity for exercise.

An important part of caring correctly for the birds is the keeper's behavior towards his charges. He should move calmly when he approaches them, avoiding abrupt movements. He should also avoid wearing anything conspicuous the birds are not familiar with. Thus a hat, for example, which has suddenly appeared on the head of a person the animals have otherwise grown to trust can cause an outbreak of terrible panic among all the birds.

The great majority of parrots are very gregarious birds which, unlike a chaffinch or even a canary, are only happy, when kept on their own, if the keeper gives them a lot of attention throughout the day. Where this is not possible, individual birds should not be kept. It would be wrong to keep a bird purely for its ornamental value. Primarily, the single parrot needs to get used to its keeper. It must be treated not only calmly but with extra affection as well, and the first thing it needs to get used to is the keeper's hand. With the help of all sorts of treats, this usually does not present too much of a problem. When selecting a bird, make sure to get a young one. Old parrots often prove unruly.

Opposite: A pair of Jandaya Conures. Proper perches are vital to the health of all parrots. The birds will use them to exercise the muscles of the feet and to help sharpen the beaks.

A Black Parrot.
Bright eyes
and clean, tight
plumage are
signs of good
health in
parrots.

*"The most talented
[talkers] are the
Grey Parrot, the
Amazons, the
Senegal Parrot,
and the* Ara
species."

and tend to resist all efforts to tame them. The use of force achieves absolutely nothing.

Once the parrot has grown tame, the keeper can try to teach it to talk, to sing songs, or to whistle tunes or signals. To teach a bird to talk, the word it is meant to learn should be repeated clearly, as often as possible, and always in the same tone of voice. One should not go on to the next stage until the animal has learned a word properly. Otherwise there is a danger that it will get everything mixed up. The ability to mimic human speech varies considerably not only within the parrot family but

also among individuals of any particular species. The most talented are the Grey Parrot, the Amazons, the Senegal Parrot, and the *Ara* species. But other parrots sometimes show considerable talent, too. Take the little Budgerigar, for instance, which for all its diminutive size can be a great "orator" at times. Then again, one can get birds that learn little or nothing, and all the trouble one takes with these is so much wasted effort since they are totally lacking in talent.

The learning capacity of the males is nearly always greater than that of the females. But the keeper comes into it, too. Parrots which for some inexplicable reason have an antipathy to their keeper can be neither tamed nor trained by the latter. It is best to part from the animal under these circumstances, as one is unlikely to derive much pleasure from it. Another well-known fact is that some parrots show a greater affinity for persons of the female sex while others prefer the male sex. It is not, however, the case, as Brehm maintained, that birds are able to differentiate clearly between men and women; and Dr. Th. Zell, whom I remember from my student days when he greatly impressed me with his "crossing-over rule," was also mistaken when he said that "a female animal tends to attach itself more to a man and a male animal more to a woman." Nevertheless it is true that there are "ladies' birds" among the parrots, i.e., individuals which respond only to women, as well as "gentlemen's birds" which prefer men. The explanation for this undoubtedly is that the "ladies' birds" were reared by a female person and the "gentlemen's birds" by a person of the male gender.

Even if parrots receive the best care possible, they can sometimes become ill—catch a chill, for instance, and suffer from a runny nose or a cough, or get an upset tummy due to eating some food or other that does not entirely agree with them. The over-anxious bird fancier will then almost invariably think of psittacosis—the disease which has received such a lot of publicity—purely because the patient happens to be a parrot. If some other species of bird were involved he would never dream of suspecting psittacosis, even though it is a proven fact that other species, too—among them canaries, domestic pigeons, poultry, and ducks—can be carriers of the psittacosis (or more precisely, the ornithosis) virus. I am

not disputing that caution is always advisable where a parrot has fallen ill, but one should not panic and jump to conclusions, either. Even a parrot can suffer from an "ordinary" cold or cough or from "normal" diarrhea that can be treated with the usual remedies. The scope of this book does not permit me to discuss the individual diseases and their treatment.

A pair of Illiger's Macaws. Smaller Macaws may be kept in spacious cages of at least 1.5 m in length.

"[A] well-known fact is that some parrots show a greater affinity for persons of the female sex while others prefer the male sex."

A Mallee Ringneck Parrot. If possible, offer your parrots perches with a variety of diameters so that the feet will not have to hold the same grip.

Species of Parrots

"*Parrotlets of the genus* Forpus *are small birds, roughly the size of finches, with a bright green plumage and, where the males are concerned, blue or yellow markings.*"

A male Barred Parakeet. This species is pleasant and easy to feed, but it is rather sensitive to cold weather.

FAMILY ARATINGIDAE

This family embraces all the American parrots, including some 145 species which have become extinct in relatively recent times. Some are long-tailed, like the Macaws and the smaller wedge-tailed parakeets, others short-tailed like the Amazons. The different groups, here treated as subfamilies, are often difficult to differentiate, however, since there are species that occupy an intermediate position as regards appearance. From the Old World family of Grey Parrots, these New World parrots are distinguished by certain behavioral characteristics, and despite some similarities it is not certain whether the two families are particularly closely related. Perhaps the parrotlets of the genus *Forpus* which, in their build and behavior bear a slight resemblance to the Australian Lories, are the most primitive of the New World parrots.

Subfamily Forpinae Parrotlets of the genus *Forpus* are small birds, roughly the size of finches, with a bright green plumage and, where the males are concerned, blue or yellow markings. Special characteristics are not only the minute size but also the stout, laterally thickened bill, the long, tapered wings which extend almost to the tip of the tail, and the short, wedge-shaped tail whose individual feathers are pointed. Parrotlets are found from northwestern Mexico to South America. Within this range they occur in five species with about 15 races southward as far as Paraguay and northeastern Argentina. They live gregariously in small to very large flocks and in some areas are as numerous as sparrows. They can be found particularly on shrubs and trees and feed on the latter's blossoms, berries, fruits, and shoots. In captivity they receive millet, canary seed, and sunflower seeds. Hemp has to be given with caution. Suitable raising-foods are biscuits, ant pupae, and mealworms, although many birds do not, in fact, touch these foods. Parrotlets readily adapt to free flight.

Usually only three forms are available on the market. The first of these is the Turquoise-rumped, Blue-rumped, or Mexican Parrotlet (*Forpus cyanopygius*) from western Mexico, of which there are three different races. In the females, the rump is not blue but green. This parrotlet measures about 13 cm in length.

Of the Green-rumped Parrotlet (*Forpus passerinus*), 11 races are

A pair of Celestial Parrots. Celestial Parrots, and other species of parrotlets, sometimes show an ability for speech.

A beautiful Green-winged Macaw, a species which looks like the commonly imported Scarlet Macaw. Note the green wings on this crimson bird.

Covert: a feather that covers the base of a quill on the tail and on the wings.

known. Their range consists of a large part of South America, southward to Paraguay and northeastern Argentina. Plumage is green; underside yellowish green, rump green.

Among the parrotlets which more recently have been appearing on the bird market again (at least occasionally) is the Celestial, or Pacific or Lesson's Parrotlet (*Forpus coelestis*). It lives in western Ecuador and western Peru, and attains a length of 12 cm. Plumage is green; the anterior and sides of the head are yellowish green, as is the throat; back grayish green, neck light blue; rump, secondaries, primary coverts blue in the male, whereas the female, which is slightly bigger, does not possess any blue feathers.

Parrotlets are wild and shy initially but gradually quiet down, although always remaining reserved and cautious. Young birds, on the other hand, grow tame and confiding, although they, too, do not like anyone to get excessively close. When excited, their voice is a shrill

shrieking. At other times they utter a rather pleasant twittering. Generally speaking, parrotlets behave peaceably towards other birds, except during the breeding season. They are widely bred in captivity. Suitable nestboxes are the ones normally used for Budgerigars, i.e., the tall ones, not the horizontal design. The clutch consists of four to five eggs, on an average, which take about 19 to 21 days to mature. The young leave the nestbox at the age of 30 to 33 days. Parrotlets can be kept in an unheated room in the winter. These miniatures have also been known to demonstrate an ability to talk.

As a particularly endearing representative of the genus *Bolborhynchus*, the Barred Parakeet (*Bolborhynchus lineola*) deserves to be mentioned here. Its three races are distributed over southern Mexico through Central America to Colombia, Peru, and northwestern Venezuela, where their habitat is the mountains. This small, appealing, and peace-loving parakeet attains a length of 17 cm, one-third of which is taken up by the tail. The basic color is green. The feathers on the upper parts, neck, and flanks have black margins. The median tail feathers are black near the ends. The beak is of a light horny yellow. The feet are brownish. The Barred Parakeet—frequently imported in the past, nowadays only seldom on the market—does not shriek but utters a soft, pleasing twitter. It is peaceable and makes no special demands on the keeper. It is, however, sensitive to cold. Although it has been bred in captivity on several occasions, it is not all that easy to match a pair since the sexes are almost impossible to distinguish by their external characteristics. The female is said to be slightly smaller. Suitable food for this parakeet consists mainly of millet and canary seed, with fruit in addition. It also

Hyacinth and Green-winged Macaws. In the wild, Green-winged Macaws often live in pairs or small groups rather than in large flocks.

"Despite the comparatively plain coloration of its plumage, the Sierra Parakeet is well worth keeping. It is not only elegant in build but is also peaceable and . . . undemanding."

likes biscuits. Greenstuff should, of course, be offered as well whenever possible, and fresh twigs for gnawing must be made available at all times.

The genus *Amoropsittaca* consists of a single species, the Sierra Parakeet (*Amoropsittaca aymara*), which has appeared on the market from time to time in recent years. This small parakeet, measuring about 21 to 22 cm in length, is found in the highlands of Bolivia and Argentina. Its basic color is green, the crown, eye region, and ear coverts are dark brown, the cheeks, sides of the neck, and the throat pale gray. The two sexes are more or less identical in color, except that in the female the crown, eye region, and ear coverts are more brownish gray, i.e., lighter than in the male. The hen also happens to be slightly smaller. Despite the comparatively plain coloration of its plumage, the Sierra Parakeet is well worth keeping. It is not only elegant in

build but is also a peaceable and, on the whole, an undemanding bird which does not scream but utters an unobtrusive twittering or chatter.

The Sierra Parakeet is an agile flier and should, therefore, be kept in a really spacious cage or, better still, in an aviary. It is not choosy where its food is concerned. It should be offered millet, canary seed, and oats, as well as sunflower seeds, grass seeds in a semi-mature condition, and plenty of greenstuff. A wide variety of nuts is gratefully accepted, too, as is fruit. The Sierra Parakeet has repeatedly been bred in captivity with good success. The raising-food consists of a soft-food mixture. The kind of nestbox normally used for Budgerigars is adequate. This can also serve as a roosting-place. Sierra Parakeets enjoy bathing.

Subfamily Aratinginae This group hails from the warmer regions of South America. These parrots have a wedge-shaped tail—long in

Sierra Parakeets are peaceful, quiet, and undemanding. They also enjoy taking baths and eating nuts.

the majority of species—all the feathers of which are arranged in steps of varying length, and, to a greater or lesser extent, narrowing towards the apex. The basic plumage color of most species, apart from a few large Macaws, is green, and there is virtually no difference between the sexes. All parrots of this group are highly gregarious, many species during the breeding season as well. They are nimble fliers and agile climbers but tend to be clumsy on the ground. They have a shrieking voice. The diet consists of all sorts of grass seeds, berries, and fruit. Many species, however, accept insects as well. A great many species have have proven to be undemanding and long-lived pets in captivity.

Unfortunately, they are very noisy in the early stages. They also do a lot of gnawing, which means they can only be kept in metal cages. Since they like plenty of exercise, the cage needs to be spacious, too. For

"[Macaws] are nimble fliers and agile climbers but tend to be clumsy on the ground. . . .A great many species have proven to be undemanding and long-lived pets in captivity."

A Yellow-collared Macaw, a species that is slightly smaller than Illiger's Macaw.

"Kept on their own, some [Macaw] species grow extraordinarily tame within a short period, learn to imitate words and even whole sentences, and to whistle tunes."

A Chestnut-fronted Macaw, one of the smaller species of Macaw.

smaller species its length should be at least 1.5m. The larger Macaws cannot be kept in cages at all but only in aviaries or free on climbing trees and T-stands. Many species are unsuitable for mixed housing, as they sometimes, with their beaks, injure the legs. They are great gnawers, which means they must have fresh twigs at their disposal at all times, else they will attack any and all wooden furnishings such as perches, nestboxes, etc. They are fed on millet, canary seed, hemp, oats, fruit and berries, to which maize, sunflower seeds, and various nuts are added where the larger species are concerned. That the diet is supplemented with all kinds of greenstuff goes without saying. A few species have been successfully bred in captivity. Kept on their own, some species grow extraordinarily tame within a short period, learn to imitate words and even whole sentences, and to whistle tunes.

As representatives of the three species that make up the genus *Anodorhynchus*, I should just like to mention the Hyacinth Macaw (*Anodorhynchus hyacinthinus*) here,

which, with its total length of up to 98 cm, is the largest parrot. Individual specimens come on the market fairly regularly. The color of the plumage, in both sexes, is a beautiful cobalt blue, of a slightly lighter shade on the head and neck, dark on the crown, nape, wings, and tail. The bare eyering, as well as a bare border around the lower mandible, is golden yellow. The powerful bill is black, the feet are blackish, the eyes dark brown.

The home of the Hyacinth Macaw is Brazil, south of the Amazon in the states of Para, Piaui, Goias, Minas Gerais, São Paulo, and Mato Grosso.

The genus *Ara* embraces a large number of very big as well as smaller species whose main characteristic is that, as opposed to the Hyacinth Macaw, they are bare and unfeathered not only in the eye region but also on the sides of the head or at least on the cheeks.

Illiger's Macaw (*Ara maracana*), 44 cm long and native to eastern Brazil,

from the Ilha de Marajó to the Rio Grande do Sul, and to Paraguay and Misiones in Argentina, is a comparatively rare occurrence on the market. Here, the basic color is green, the forehead red, head bluish, rump, upper tail coverts olive green, with a scarlet spot on the lower back and belly, blue primary coverts and wings. The bare cheeks are flesh-colored. Its small size alone makes Illiger's Macaw an ideal pet in the home.

Closely related to the latter is the Yellow-collared Macaw (*Ara auricollis*) which has recently started to appear on the bird market. It originates from northwestern Argentina, Bolivia, Paraguay, and Mato Grosso in Brazil. It is still smaller than Illiger's Macaw, dark green with a blackish brown forehead, a tinge of blue on the crown, a golden yellow band round the neck, blue wings, and a tail that is blue above at the tip, otherwise brownish red. The bare cheeks are yellowish.

A length of 45 to 52 cm has the Chestnut-fronted Macaw (*Ara severa*), of which there are two races. These are distributed from the Orinoco over Guyana, eastern Panama, Colombia, Ecuador, and Bolivia. The basic color of this small Macaw is a dark grass green. The upper parts are more olive green, the band on the forehead and the edges of the cheeks and chin dark reddish brown; the lesser under wing coverts and the edges of the wings red, primaries blue, secondaries green on the outside; tail feathers reddish brown with blue tips; the beak

Primaries: the longest feathers on the wing of a bird.

Due to their beautiful plumage and large size, Macaws are especially striking parrots.

A Military Macaw, a species which has three different races.

"[The Scarlet Macaw] is one of the most frequently imported Macaws."

A cluster of Blue and Yellow Macaws. These birds are frequently imported and are said to be very gifted speakers.

black, likewise the feet, the iris yellow. In the past, individual Chestnut-fronted Macaws were available on the bird market at regular intervals, and in recent years they have appeared again from time to time. In behavior the species is much like its large relatives. There have been several successful breeding attempts in captivity.

With a length of about 78 to 90 cm, the Scarlet Macaw (*Ara macao*) is roughly twice the size of the two species just mentioned. It is distributed from tropical Mexico over Central and South America to eastern Ecuador, eastern Peru, Bolivia, and Brazil in the states of Amazonas and Para to northern Mato Grosso. It is one of the most frequently imported Macaws.

From eastern Panama southward

A Brown-throated Conure. In the wild, these birds are often found in local villages and surrounding areas, as they are quite tame and unafraid of humans.

The plumage of the Brown-throated Conure is relatively unassuming, especially when compared to that of some of its close relatives.

to Bolivia, Argentinian Chaco, Paraguay, Misiones, and Parana extends the range of the equally large Green-winged Macaw (*Ara chloroptera*). The basic color of its plumage is a dark scarlet. Wings and primary coverts, upper and under tail coverts, as well as the tips of the tail feathers light blue; the feathers on the shoulders and the median wing coverts green; under wing coverts, feathers of the nape and mantle red with green margins, several rows of small red feathers on the bare cheeks; upper mandible of a pale horny color, lower mandible black, the feet blackish, the eyes straw-colored. This large Macaw, which externally looks very similar to the Scarlet Macaw, is also imported quite frequently.

Buffon's Macaw (*Ara ambigua*), of which there are two races, occurs in Nicaragua, Costa Rica, Panama, and Colombia. It measures 80 to 85 cm in length. Plumage is yellowish green, forehead scarlet; rump, upper tail coverts light blue; greater wing coverts, outer vanes of wings and under tail coverts blue; tail feathers

reddish brown with blue tips. Considerably smaller, at a length of 62.5 to 65 cm, is the Military Macaw (*Ara militaris*), of which three races with only very little difference between them are found in Mexico. Its range also extends to Colombia and as far as northwestern Venezuela, as well as covering Ecuador and northern Peru and Bolivia to as far as the Argentinian border. The color of its plumage is not yellowish green like that of Buffon's Macaw but grass green. Forehead scarlet, mantle sky blue, back and shoulders of a faded-looking olive-brown color; the bare cheeks of a pale flesh-color, with four narrow rows of purplish brown feathers; beak black, feet blackish, eyes yellowish gray. There is no difference between the two sexes where the color of the plumage is concerned.

One of the largest and most frequently imported Macaws is the Blue and Yellow Macaw (*Ara ararauna*). It has a total length of 80 to 96.5 cm, with the tail making up about 50 cm of this. The Blue and

Orange-fronted Conures, parrots which grow tame rather quickly but which are uncommon in captivity.

Mandibles: the upper and lower parts of a bird's beak, comparable to a human's upper and lower jaw.

A Red- masked Conure.

A pair of Cactus Conures.

"The Blue and Yellow Macaw is one of the most beautiful Macaws. As regards learning ability, it is undoubtedly the most gifted of them all. . . ."

A Brown-throated Conure, a species which frequently grows confiding.

Yellow Macaw is one of the most beautiful Macaws. As regards learning ability, it is undoubtedly the most gifted of them all—able to imitate words and whole sentences distinctly and loudly. It grows extraordinarily tame. There have been several successful breeding attempts in captivity. The number of eggs per clutch range from two to six. The incubation period spans about 30 days, and the young leave the nest at the age of about three months. The species has been successfully crossed with the Green-winged Macaw. The Blue and Yellow Macaw is native to tropical South America, from eastern Panama to Ecuador, eastern Peru, Bolivia, northern Paraguay, and Brazil. In Brazil its range extends southward to São Paulo and Rio de Janeiro.

The Blue and Yellow Macaw happens to be one of the first parrots brought back to Europe alive.

All Macaws are native to tropical America, where they occur predominantly in the rain forests of the lowlands and feed on all sorts of seeds and fruit. They also take cereals and maize, however, which means they can cause considerable damage in agricultural areas.

The beak of the Macaws is extraordinarily strong. The upper mandible, with its pointed tip, is sharply curved downward and has a distinct notch. The lower mandible is taller and truncated. The wings are long and facilitate rapid flight. Macaws are nimble climbers; on the ground, however, they stalk sideways and look rather clumsy. They are gregarious birds which often assemble in huge flocks. In accordance with their size, their voice is loud and unpleasantly shrill. They nest inside the hollows of trees, which they also use outside of the breeding season. The clutch is comprised of two eggs which are comparatively round and, like those of all parrots, white in color. The plumage colors of the Macaws are identical in the two sexes.

In captivity, Macaws are fed on wild seeds, oats, maize, sunflower seeds, hemp, and nuts such as

walnuts, hazelnuts, peanuts, and pinenuts. White bread or rusks are popular. In addition they should be given greenstuff, ripe fruit, and carrots. Fresh twigs for gnawing must be provided at all times.

Macaws are talented talkers and, if treated right, lovable, tame, and affectionate birds. If trained properly and treated well, they will never attack their keeper with their beak. Just how much strength there is in a Macaw's beak can be seen when the bird cracks a hard peach stone (for instance), apparently without the slightest effort. The peach stone is pressed against the upper mandible with the tongue, which broadens anteriorly like a piston, and is moved about and turned over until it is suitably positioned. Then the lower mandible is put to it like a chisel. Strong pressure is applied just once, and the peach stone breaks in half. The two halves are allowed to drop to the ground, whereas their contents—the small, almond-like kernel—is devoured. So, caution is advisable when it comes to the beak of a Macaw one does not know! It does not require much effort on the bird's part to bite clean through a finger. They may even cut through the chain by which they are tethered to the stand if the former is of insufficient thickness. Macaws are usually kept on a parrot stand such as we are all familiar with from our visits to zoological gardens. Just how beautiful these big birds really are only becomes fully apparent, however, when they are kept in complete freedom, without any fetters whatsoever. Thus it was still possible a few years ago to admire free-flying Macaws of various species at the Cologne Zoo and in the well-known Dutch bird park "Avifauna."

Red on the forehead, cheeks, and shoulders, otherwise green, is the Red-masked Conure (*Psittacara erythrogenys*), from western Ecuador and western Peru, which is imported from time to time.

A pretty bird with striking colors is the Jandaya Conure (*Aratinga solstitialis jandaya*), one of the four subspecies of the Sun Conure (*Aratinga solstitialis*), which occurs in

Guyana as well as in the Rio Branco range in northwestern Brazil. It has a length of 30 to 32.5 cm, and the tail is 13 to 15.5 cm long. As opposed to related species, this bird has proved to be of fairly peaceable disposition and can thus be kept in association with other birds. Kept on its own, it grows very tame and can sometimes learn to mimic a few words as well. A tamed Jandaya only seldom makes its shrill and rather unpleasant voice heard. The Jandaya Conure has repeatedly been bred in captivity. In recent years hybrids have been produced by crossing the Nanday Conure with the Jandaya and Jandaya Conure with the Cactus Conure.

A highly recommended pet which quickly grows tame but, unfortunately, does not appear on the market very often is the Orange-fronted Conure (*Eupsittula canicularis*). Its two races are found on the Pacific coast from the Istmo de Tehuantepec to Costa Rica and in western Mexico. It has a length of 25 cm. The plumage is green, the forehead red, the crown grayish blue, the sides of the head and the throat olive-brown, breast, belly, and under wing coverts yellowish green, beak whitish.

The Brown-throated Conure (*Eupsittula pertinax*) is distributed from western Panama to the Amazon range and Guyana. One of its 14 races that has been imported is *Eupsittula pertinax aeruginosa*, from northern Colombia and northwestern Venezuela. It has a length of 25 cm. This Conure, like the previous one, is a bird of a fairly unassuming coloration. The basic color is green, the crown grayish blue, the cheeks and throat olive-yellow. Like the Orange-fronted Conure, however, it grows very tame and confiding.

The same applies to the Cactus Conure (*Eupsittula cactorum*), whose two races are distributed over northeastern Brazil. This bird is also similar in size to the two Conures just mentioned. Its plumage color is green, the crown bluish, the forehead olive-brown, the throat yellowish brown, breast and belly orange-yellow. As already stated when discussing the Jandaya Conure, hybrids have been produced by crossing the Jandaya with the Cactus Conure.

Slightly bigger, with a length of 28 cm, is the Peach-fronted Conure (*Eupsittula aurea*), whose two races occur in Brazil, mainly south of the Amazon and east of the Rio Madeira as far as eastern Bolivia, northwestern Argentina (Salta), Mato Grosso, São Paulo, and Paraguay. The Peach-fronted Conure has the same pleasant characteristics as the three preceding species. It quickly grows tame and confiding and also learns to talk quite well. Breeding in captivity has repeatedly been successful. The nestbox should be about 28 to 30 by 17 to 25 cm, with an entrance hole of 5 to 7 cm. The clutch consists of two eggs,

Opposite: A pair of Painted Conures. The Painted Conure is quite common in most parts of its range except northern Colombia.

Crown: consists of the feathers on top of the bird's head, usually confined to the area between and above the eyes.

The Maroon-bellied Conure has been successfully hybridized with the White-eared Conure.

Nanday Conures are frequently found in captivity and make good pets. They do, however, have a loud, raucous voice.

Hybridization: cross-breeding between birds of different species, often carried out in captivity and occasionally occurring in nature where the territories of two similar species overlap.

incubation period 26 days; male and female take the incubating in turn. The young leave the nest at the age of 50 days.

The sole species of the genus *Conuropsis* and at the same time the only parrot of northern America is or, rather, was the Carolina Peroquet *(Conuropsis carolinensis)*. The race *Conuropsis carolinensis carolinensis* occurred in the southeastern U.S.A. from southern Virginia to Florida, and the other one, *Conuropsis carolinensis ludovicianus*, the Louisiana Peroquet, in the Mississippi range. The last hour of this parrot came when its native rain forests were cleared. The birds had, in any case, already been subject to intense persecution on account of the damage they were doing to fruit plantations. Both races became increasingly rare, and the last Carolina Peroquets were sighted in Florida in 1904, while the only remaining Louisiana Peroquet died ten years later as a cagebird.

With its green basic color, yellow head, orange-red forehead and eye

region, the Carolina Peroquet was an exceedingly attractive parrot, and it is interesting to note that it was one of the most common parrots on the bird market. It measured 35 cm in length. The fact that breeding this species in captivity presented no problem and that, furthermore, it was hardy and even tolerated severe cold makes it seem rather strange that it did not prove possible to save this parrot from extinction by continuing its propagation in captivity.

Fairly well-known is the Nanday Conure *(Nandayus nenday)*, whose native range extends from southeastern Bolivia and southern Mato Grosso to the upper Pilcomayo, Argentinian Chaco, and Paraguay. The Nanday Conure is available on the market at fairly frequent intervals. It makes quite a pleasant pet, with the drawback, however, that it calls in a loud and shrill voice. It does not cause excessive damage to wood. Attempts to breed it in captivity have been successful, as has hybridization with the Jandaya Conure. The incubation period spans 25 days, and the young fledge at the age of about seven weeks. It measures 30 to 33 cm in length.

The small, slender conures of the genus *Pyrrhura* are distinguished by the reddish brown coloration of the whole, or part of, the underside of the tail. There are approximately 17 species.

The three races of the Maroon-bellied Conure (*Pyrrhura frontalis*) are distributed over southeastern Brazil, Uruguay, northern Argentina, and Paraguay. This species is green, pale grayish brown in the ear region, on the throat and breast, the latter having dark crossbands. There is a dark red spot on the belly and a narrow, dark brownish red band on the forehead. The length of this bird is 28 cm.

A dainty, fairly active bird that grows tame is the White-eared Conure (*Pyrrhura leucotis*). It is split into five races whose range embraces Venezuela and large parts of eastern Brazil. It, too, has a green basic color. The crown is grayish brown, the nape light blue; a narrow reddish brown band on the forehead. Eye

Nape: the area on the back of the bird's neck.

Head study of a Nanday Conure. It is said that the wild Nanday has benefited from land settlement, as it feeds on sunflower and maize crops.

Ear coverts: feathers on the bird's head which are located behind and below the eye region and above the cheek.

region and cheeks reddish brown. The ear coverts are whitish gray. The feathers on the throat are gray with whitish borders. There is a brownish red spot on the belly, shoulders red, rump brownish red. The species measures a mere 22 cm in length. The tail is 10 cm long.

The White-eared Conure, more frequently imported in the past, has been bred in captivity a few times. It has also been successfully crossed with the Maroon-bellied Conure.

The Painted Conure (*Pyrrhura picta*), which attains a length of 24 cm, is distributed over Venezuela, Guyana, Surinam, Cayenne, Colombia, eastern Peru, and northern Brazil, spreading southward to northern Mato Grosso and Goias. There are seven races. Again the basic color is green. Crown and nape brown; forehead and lower cheeks grayish blue, likewise a band on the neck; lower neck brown, the individual feathers having a light border; belly cherry red in the center; lower back, rump, upper tail coverts, and tail also cherry red.

One subspecies of the Painted Conure, which has been making an

Maroon-bellied Conure. This parrot is very noisy when in flight but is silent when feeding in the tree tops.

Painted Conures, like birds of other *Pyrrhura* species, require twigs and branches for chewing at all times.

appearance on the market in recent years and was available in the past as well, is *Pyrrhura picta lucianii*, whose range extends from eastern Peru to northwestern Brazil. It has a red crown and a red stripe on the forehead. The eye region, lores, and cheeks are also red.

Pyrrhura species are fed on millet, canary seed, oats, cooked rice and maize, as well as on half-ripened grass seeds. They also need all kinds of greenstuff and fruit. Because of their gnawing requirements, fresh twigs should not be absent. Painted

Conures are pleasant pets and in the aviary usually get on well with birds of other species, too.

On the eastern slopes of the Andes from western Argentina to Tierra del Fuego as well as in Chile we find the two races of the Austral Conure (*Enicognathus ferrugineus*), a large bird with a length of 33 cm. Its basic plumage color is green, the underside more olive green, all feathers with blackish borders. Forehead, belly, vent, tail feathers copper red, the latter greenish at the tips. There have been occasional

Lores: the area between the eyes and the beak of a bird.

The Canary-winged Parakeet has a pleasant disposition and does not have an over-developed urge to chew.

"Properly treated. . . [Monk Parakeets] gradually quiet down and grow tame, and they make rather pleasant pets that even show a talent for talking."

A blue mutation of the Monk Parakeet. Monk Parakeets are well-known for their loud screaming, which can be eliminated with proper acclimatization and patient taming sessions.

imports of this species.

Deviating slightly from the other members of this subfamily is the sole species of the genus *Myiopsitta,* the Monk Parakeet (*Myiopsitta monachus*). It is always available on the market and, therefore, likely to be known to everyone. Its native range is central Argentina to Uruguay, Bolivia and southern Brazil. It has a length of 27 to 30 cm, the tail measures 11.5 to 14.8 cm. Plumage color is green. Forehead, throat, cheeks, and breast are ash gray. Wings, primary coverts blue, with a narrow green margin. Beak a light yellowish gray, feet brownish gray. The sexes are identical in color. Imported Monk Parakeets are predominantly older birds that have been caught in the wild; they are shy and unruly and are unpleasant screamers in the bargain. Properly treated, however, they gradually quiet down and grow tame, and then make rather pleasant pets that even show a talent for talking. They are undemanding and

The Monk
Parakeet is
difficult to
tame if it is not
obtained as a
young bird.

The Canary-winged Parakeet has a pleasant, agreeable disposition. Large flocks of these birds live together until the breeding season, when they break up into pairs.

hardy and can be left outdoors without reservation in the winter months. Because of their great gnawing urge, they need to be housed in a strong metal cage. They can be kept in association with other parrots, but not with smaller ones or other kinds of birds.

The Monk Parakeet has frequently been bred in captivity. It is the only parrot which does not breed inside hollows but uses twigs to build a free-standing large, spherical nest with an entrance from below or at the side. Several pairs may join up to build a large nest with several breeding chambers and a common entrance. Depending on the number of pairs involved, a nest of this type can measure two meters or more in diameter. Monk Parakeets quickly become accustomed to free flight. It must be borne in mind, however, that their loud screaming can turn them into a nuisance and that they can cause considerable damage by plundering fruit trees, not even sparing the twigs which, of course, they require for nest-building.

Prior to World War II, the Berlin Zoo owned a large flight of free-flying Monk Parakeets, which had built their extensive nest from twigs in the garden and raised a number of broods every year. On one occasion, the young included a yellow bird which was trapped and transferred to the new pheasant enclosure where it survived for many years. As far as I know, this yellow Monk Parakeet never produced any progeny, which is rather a pity.

Very recently a pair of blue Monk Parakeets were offered on the bird market for the first time.

Subfamily Brotogeryinae In representatives of this group, the beak is laterally compressed, the ridge narrow and as tall as it is long, the tip of the beak long and thin and strongly curved downward, the lower mandible extended. The wings

are long and pointed, the tail is wedge-shaped, the feathers arranged in steps. The tarsus is short, the toes weak. The sexes are identical in coloration. The basic color of the plumage is green. The Brotogeryinae are native to South America; the range of one species extends to southern Mexico.

The genus *Brotogeris* includes some very nice and appealing birds, which grow extraordinarily tame and

A trio of Orange-chinned Parakeets. These birds are somewhat more delicate than other members of their genus, but once acclimatized, they make wonderful pets.

"The genus Brotogeris includes some very nice and appealing birds, which grow extraordinarily tame and confiding once they have lost their initial shyness."

The Grey-cheeked Parakeet grows quite tame and is a very popular cage bird in its native South America. It is also quite popular with parrot fanciers around the world.

Median feathers: the central feathers on the tail of the bird.

confiding once they have lost their initial shyness. The voice is less loud as a rule, not becoming a nuisance. They are peaceable and can, therefore, be kept in association with smaller birds.

The Plain Parakeet (*Brotogeris tirica*) occurs in eastern and southern Brazil. It measures 25 to 26 cm in length, the tail 10 to 12.5 cm. The plumage is green, of a lighter yellowish green on the forehead, sides of the head, and underside.

The primaries and primary coverts are blue, the former with a narrow green border on the outside. The tail is green, the median feathers of a faded-looking bluish color; a flesh-colored beak. This parakeet is a popular cagebird in its native range and was also frequently imported in the past. Unfortunately, it is a terrible screamer. On the other hand, it is an undemanding and hardy pet which can be left in unheated rooms in the winter.

The Plain Parakeet is undemanding and hardy, but it can be a terrible screamer.

Tui Parakeets, like other members of the genus *Brotogeris,* should always be kept with another parrot, as they do not fare very well on their own.

The Golden-winged Parakeet comes in three races and has the shortest length of any member of its genus.

Unlike the *Brotogeris* species, Amazon Parrots are gnawers. This is a Red-lored Amazon.

Chin: the region located under the bird's beak, just above the throat.

Breeding attempts have been successful.

Of roughly the same size as the Plain Parakeet is the Canary-winged Parakeet (*Brotogeris chiriri*), which some taxonomists classify as *Brotogeris versicolorus chiriri*, i.e., a subspecies of *Brotogeris versicolorus*. In the Canary-winged Parakeet, too, the basic color of the plumage is green, of a lighter shade below. The primaries and the greater coverts, with the exception of the inner ones, are yellow. The beak is of a light horn-color, the feet are flesh-colored. This parakeet grows very tame and shows a pleasing disposition. Its screaming can make it a bit of a nuisance, however. There is no excessive gnawing where this species is concerned. The birds

like climbing. Their native range extends from Bolivia and eastern Brazil to northern Argentina and Paraguay.

The Grey-cheeked Parakeet (*Brotogeris pyrrhopterus*) comes from Ecuador and northwestern Peru. It has a length of 20 to 22 cm. Its plumage is green above, forehead, sides of the head, chin pale gray, crown a light blue green, greater wing coverts and primaries dark blue, under wing coverts orange, beak of a light flesh-color, likewise the feet. Like the Canary-wing, the Grey-cheeked Parakeet grows extraordinarily tame. Usually it is already in a tamed condition when it reaches us, since it is as popular a cagebird in its native range as its relatives. Not infrequently, the new arrivals mount the hand without any qualms. They learn to speak a few words.

By and large, what has already been said also applies to the Orange-chinned Parakeet *(Brotogeris jugularis)*, which is distributed from southwestern Mexico to northern Colombia and northern Venezuela.

feathers show a tinge of blue. The beak is of a light horn gray, feet of a gray flesh-color. The Orange-chinned Parakeet has shown itself to be somewhat delicate and in need of warmth in the early stages, but if carefully looked after, it acclimatizes well and keeping it then presents no problems. It likes to spend the night

Profile of a Yellow-lored Amazon. The Yellow-lored Amazon is sometimes confused with the White-fronted Amazon, to whom it is closely related.

With a length of 18 to 19.5 cm it is still smaller than the Grey-cheeked. The plumage color consists of different shades of green. There is a light orange-yellow spot on the chin. The lesser wing coverts are olive-brown. The primary coverts are deep blue, the under wing coverts yellow. The tail is green, its median

inside a box. It also learns to mimic a few words. Several successful breeding attempts have been reported.

From the lower range of the Amazon comes the Tuipara Parakeet *(Brotogeris chrysopterus tuipara),* one of the three races of the Golden-winged Parakeet *(Brotogeris*

"The Orange-chinned Parakeet. . .if carefully looked after. . . acclimatizes well. . . .It also learns to mimic a few words."

"The Tui Parakeet is an exceedingly nice, lovable, and peaceable little parrot, and with its pleasant disposition gives a lot of pleasure to its keeper."

chrysopterus) which is distributed over northeastern South America. The Tuipara Parakeet attains a length of 19 to 20 cm. The overall plumage color is green. The edge of the forehead, a spot on the chin, and the primary coverts are orange. Primaries blackish blue, beak horn white, feet flesh-colored. In disposition, etc., it is very much like its relatives.

The last member of the genus I would like to mention here is the Tui Parakeet (*Brotogeris*

sanctithomae), whose two races are native to northwestern Brazil, northeastern Peru, and the lower range of the Amazon. The species grows to 17 to 18.3 cm in length and is the smallest of the genus.

The Tui Parakeet is an exceedingly nice, loveable, and peaceable little parrot, and with its pleasant disposition gives a lot of pleasure to its keeper. I still have very fond memories of the two Tui Parakeets (whether they were a pair I do not know, since the sexes look alike

A White-bellied Caique. In the wild this species feeds on fruits, seeds, and berries.

externally) I had in my care until just before the War. Like many other species that are popular cagebirds in their country of origin, these two Tuis came into my possession with their wings clipped, which meant I had to keep them in the cage initially. Gradually, and with all due caution, of course, I removed the clipped feathers, which then regenerated quickly so that the animals became able to fly again and could now be allowed to fly about indoors. On one such occasion, they escaped and spent a whole day in the tops of the trees that lined the street near my flat in Berlin before I managed to recapture them with the help of several volunteers. I had these charming little parrots for a long time. They were consistently sweet-natured, no screamers, and inseparable. They were always perched close together. When one flew off, the other followed immediately. Unfortunately, they never showed any signs of wanting to breed.

Because of their need for company, none of the little parakeets described

above should be kept on their own. One should always get at least two birds. The partner need not necessarily be a member of the same species. They just do not like being on their own.

Subfamily Amazoninae

This group includes some of the most frequently kept and, therefore, best-known parrots, above all the true Amazon parrots or, as they are generally called, Amazons, for short (genus *Amazona*). Amazons, of which there are numerous species, are native to Central and South America, where they inhabit the forests from northern Mexico to Peru, Bolivia, and Argentina. These birds lead gregarious lives and, generally speaking, live in pairs only during the breeding season. Their diet consists of different kinds of fruit, seeds, maize, cereal, nuts, fresh shoots and buds. They nest inside hollows in trees. The clutch is comprised of two to four eggs as a rule. The young leave the nest

A Yellow-shouldered Amazon Parrot. This species is said to be the tamest of all Amazons.

"Because of their need for company, none of the little [Brotogeris] parakeets. . . should be kept on their own. . . . The partner need not necessarily be a member of the same species. They just do not like being on their own."

A Cuban Amazon.

In most juvenile parrots, the plumage is darker and less distinctive than in adult birds.

hollow after about two months.

The Amazon is characterized by a thickset body, a large, powerful beak, relatively short wings, and a short, truncated broad tail. The overall plumage color of most species is green, with blue, yellow, red, or white markings notably on the head and wings. The sexes are identical in color. In juveniles, the colors of the plumage are duller and the markings less distinct. Amazons rank among the most talented parrots. They readily learn to speak, even if the words are invariably delivered "parrot-fashion" and always in the same tone of voice, in marked contrast to the performance given by the Grey Parrot. Needless to say, there are gifted and less gifted animals among the Amazons, as among all creatures. One bird learns to talk, whistle, and sing without any great effort while another just speaks or just whistles. A third may turn out to be a dead loss, either not learning at all or with only very little skill.

"The Amazon is characterized by a thickset body, a large, powerful beak, relatively short wings, and a short, truncated broad tail."

A subspecies of the Yellow-crowned Amazon, the Panama Amazon Parrot (*Amazona ochrocephala panamensis*) is often available in pet shops.

The cage intended for an Amazon should be as spacious as possible. Tame individuals may be kept on a stand. Wherever possible, the birds should be allowed free flight indoors—under supervision, however, so that they do not wreak havoc. If there is a garden, Amazons can also be given complete freedom. At the Cologne Zoo, for example, three free-flying Amazons—i.e., a Blue-fronted Amazon, a Yellow-faced Amazon, and a Blue-cheeked Amazon—were kept alongside the Macaws.

Amazons can live to a very great age. One of the longest known Amazons is the Cuban or White-headed Amazon (*Amazona leucocephala*). Its five races occur on Cuba, Isla de Pinos, on some of the Bahamas (Great Inagua, Abaco, in the past on a few other islands as well), and on the islands of Grand Cayman, Little Cayman, and Cayman Brac.

The Yellow-shouldered Amazon (*Amazona barbadensis*) becomes one of the tamest of all the Amazons. Its two races are found in the coastal region of Venezuela and on a few of the islands off the coast. This

Amazon attains a length of 34 cm. Its plumage is green; every feather has a black margin. Forehead, lores whitish. Crown, sides of the head, chin yellowish, likewise the shoulders and thighs. The first three to four secondaries are scarlet at the base of the outer vane, forming a "mirror"; towards the tip, the color changes via green into dark indigo. The beak is of a light horn-color, the feet are light bluish gray.

The most frequently imported Amazon, hence the best known of

Vane: the web or flat, expanded portion of a feather.

A Red-necked Amazon Parrot.

A Blue-fronted Amazon Parrot, one of the parrots most frequently found on the market.

". . .there are animals of extraordinary talent among the Blue-fronted Amazons which not only acquire a wide vocabulary but also learn to whistle and sing several songs."

A pair of Lilac-crowned Amazon Parrots. Amazon Parrots have a life expectancy of 30 years, and many birds may live much longer.

all, is the Blue-fronted Amazon (*Amazona aestiva*). There are two races. *Amazona aestiva aestiva* occurs in eastern and southeastern Brazil, and *Amazona aestiva xanthopteryx* (with yellow shoulders) is distributed from Bolivia and Mato Grosso to northern Argentina. Thus the species has a wide range. It is also one of the most popular Amazons with the natives. It has a length of 35 to 41.5 cm. As far as talking is concerned, there are animals of extraordinary talent among the Blue-fronted Amazons which not only acquire a wide vocabulary but also learn to whistle and sing several songs.

Breeding attempts have been successful on several occasions. The incubation period spans 30 days, and the young leave the nest hollow at the age of about two months. On one occasion the species was successfully crossed with the Cuban Amazon.

Nine races, all fairly different, are known of the Yellow-crowned Amazon (*Amazona ochrocephala*)

which has a length of 30 to 40 cm. Plumage is green, yellowish green below, feathers having narrow blackish borders, parts of the head yellow, shoulders red in the majority of races, a red "mirror" on the wings.

The races best known to the fancier are, above all, *Amazona ochrocephala ochrocephala* (Surinam Amazon), which occurs in Colombia, Venezuela, Guyana, Surinam, and southward to as far as the Rio Bravo and the central Amazon, and *Amazonas ochrocephala oratrix* (the Great Yellow-crowned Amazon), from Mexico and Honduras, which is yellow on the head and neck. The Great Yellow-crowned has proven itself to be a quick learner and a good talker.

The Green-cheeked Amazon (*Amazona viridigenalis*) from northeastern Mexico is green, with a red forehead and a red "mirror" on each wing. On the nape the green feathers have a black border. Very similar is the Lilac-crowned Amazon (*Amazona finschi*) from western

Mexico. It is lilac on the crown and the sides of the neck, and the same color is seen on the underside, the feathers having blackish borders. The Red-lored Amazon (*Amazona autumnalis*), the four races of which are distributed from southeastern Mexico to western Ecuador and northwestern Venezuela as well as over northwestern Brazil, also has a red forehead and, depending on the race, a blue or lilac crown. *Amazona autumnalis autumnalis* (range: eastern Mexico to northern Nicaragua) has yellow cheeks. In all other respects this species resembles the preceding one.

The Red-necked Amazon (*Amazona arausiaca*) hails from the island of Dominica in the Lesser Antilles. Its basic color is green. The feathers on the upper parts have black borders. The head is blue, throat and "mirror" on wings red.

Subfamily Pionitinae The range of these parrots is tropical South America. There are two species, each consisting of two races. Parrots of this group have been imported very rarely, with perhaps only individual specimens reaching the zoological gardens and the occasional fancier. It is from the Berlin Zoo that I know the Black-headed Caique (*Pionites melanocephala*), a bird with a length of 24 cm whose range extends over northern Brazil, Guyana, Venezuela, Colombia, and Peru. The diet of these parrots is the same as that of the Amazons. They are undemanding as well as hardy. Worthy of special note is the fact that they are thoroughly playful. If several of them are kept together, they literally play about the whole time. The voice can be described as a shrill whistling.

The other species, of roughly the same size, is the White-bellied Caique (*Pionites leucogaster*), which occurs in the valley of the lower Amazon, in eastern Ecuador, and from eastern Peru to western Brazil.

"...[Caiques] are undemanding as well as hardy. Worthy of special note is that they are thoroughly playful."

Red-lored Amazon. Members of this species seem to siesta during the warmest hours of the day.

Under tail coverts: the feathers located beneath the rest of the tail feathers.

In this bird the back, wings, tail, and thighs are green, the crown and nape of a reddish yellow-brown, the sides of the head, the throat and under tail coverts yellow, the breast and belly yellowish white. There is a report of a Black-headed Caique having been successfully crossed with a White-bellied Caique.

FAMILY PSITTACIDAE

The range of this family, which has a mere 12 members, is confined to Africa and Madagascar and the islands belonging to them. In many respects they resemble the Amazons. It is not certain, however, whether they are related more closely to the latter or to the *Psittaculidae* (the next family). The three genera considered to belong to the family of Grey Parrots (*Poicephalus, Psittacus,* and *Coracopsis*) differ fairly widely from one another.

One of the nine species that make up the genus *Poicephalus* is the well-known Senegal Parrot (*Poicephalus senegalus*). The race *Poicephalus senegalus senegalus* occurs in western Africa, from Senegal to Guinea-Bissau (formerly Portuguese Guinea). Another race, which is orange-red as opposed to orange-yellow on the underside, *Poicephalus senegalus versteri,* is found on the Ivory and Gold Coast, in Togo, Upper Volta, and Nigeria. A third

A trio of Black-headed Caiques. Black-headed Caiques have been successfully crossed with White-bellied Caiques.

race, *Poicephalus senegalus mesotypus*, lives in eastern Nigeria and northern Cameroon. The Senegal Parrot attains a length of 22 to 25 cm. The sexes are impossible to distinguish.

The Senegal Parrot has the reputation of being the most amiable and most human-loving of all birds, and when I think back to the various Senegal Parrots of a relative of mine, the bird fancier E. Holtzthiem, I can only say that this description is very apt. Particularly worthy of mention are the liveliness, the deep attachment formed to humans, and the confiding nature. The Senegal Parrot also learns to speak and to whistle tunes, although its voice is a bit on the "thin" side. It is important to obtain as young an animal as possible. Old Senegal Parrots can present all sorts of unpleasant problems; they may be rather unruly and wild and, above all, can turn out to be terrible screamers. Turning such a difficult wild bird into a pleasant companion involves a lot of hard work, if indeed it proves possible at all. The Senegal Parrot has already been successfully bred in captivity.

The sole species of the genus *Psittacus* is the Grey Parrot (*Psittacus erithacus*) everyone knows and loves. The genus has the following characteristics: a relatively short, straight tail; a narrow beak, laterally compressed, with white ceres which have a round indentation below the nostril, the anterior and lower edges of which run diagonally forward to terminate in a point. The bare face is white as well. The beak is black. The eye is dark gray to black at the juvenile stage and with increasing age changes at first to a lighter gray, then to gray-yellow, and eventually to the light yellow seen in old birds.

Since the absolute embargo on the import of all parrots was lifted towards the end of 1965, the Grey Parrot has also come back onto the market in large numbers and at a

very acceptable price. Sales have, therefore, been high and are continuing to be so, as I can deduce from the countless enquiries from owners and would-be owners of Grey Parrots. The Grey Parrot's nimbus as a talking bird is considerable, and it is understandable that many people would like the experience of keeping such a linguistic genius. However, where there is a lot of light, there is also a lot of shade, and by no means is every Grey Parrot a gifted artist, nor will every bird turn out to be a pupil who is eager to learn and able to absorb everything that is being demonstrated. Individual birds vary greatly as far as talent is concerned, and total failures are also known to exist. If the bird turns out to belong in the latter category, there is nothing to be done and absolutely no point in continuing with the lessons. Before even starting to teach, however (and nowadays most Grey Parrots do come on the market "untaught"), the bird must be trained to perch on one's hand.

A White-bellied Caique. Caiques are noted for their hardiness and for their playful nature.

Cere: the waxy-looking area just above the bird's beak which contains the nostrils.

65

Grey Parrots should not be purchased once their eyes have changed color from black to yellow, as yellow eyes indicate maturity.

". . .the Grey is the only parrot with an ability to imitate human words in different tones of voice. It also has an excellent capacity for association."

This presents a problem, too, since many Grey Parrots sold nowadays turn out to be less than half-tame or totally unaccustomed to contact with human beings. Hence one must be extremely careful when buying a Grey Parrot and, whenever possible, should select a bird which does not try to hide, growl, or scream as soon as one approaches its cage.

Although it is possible that a bird which exhibits such behavior might, after very loving treatment administered with endless patience, eventually lose its shyness and perhaps even grow tame, such individuals—usually caught when old (light iris)—would appear to be rather less desirable. As K. Neunzig

so rightly said: "In their youth they did not enjoy the benefit of an education and in old age they are expected to become fit for society. Something like that seldom works out." There is also the fact that many keepers, especially those who have never had a feathered companion before, have neither the very great patience nor the skill that are required to handle this type of bird; time and time again one hears of the great disappointment suffered over the much venerated Grey Parrot when all efforts proved unavailing.

Incidentally, the Grey is the only parrot with an ability to imitate human words in different tones of voice. It also has an excellent capacity for association. That is, it is able to (purely externally) connect two events with each other—when one of them occurs, to automatically experience the other. This means the parrot can utter the words, or even sentences, it has learned in situations where they are appropriate, often convincing the novice that his Grey actually understands what it is saying. This, however, is not the case. The bird is not capable of abstract or conceptual thinking; neither the well-known behavioral scientist Prof. Koehler nor others who carried out the experiment were able, for example, to even teach what in fact were highly talented Grey Parrots to say the word "food" when feeling hungry and the word "water" when feeling thirsty. The Grey Parrots do, however, learn to whistle tunes with astonishing perfection. I know of several Greys, for instance, whose showpiece among their comprehensive repertory is the well-known march from "The Bridge over the River Kwai."

Grey Parrots can live to a great age, and many cases are known where a life span of 50 to 80 years was attained. The Grey's diet in captivity consists of millet, canary

Association: the ability to connect two external events with each other—does not involve conceptual thinking.

The Grey Parrot has an exceptional capacity for speech and a long life span. In the wild it is a shy bird that rarely allows a close approach.

Eggbread: slices of bread soaked in eggs, used primarily for breeding birds and their young.

seed, oats, maize, sunflower seeds, with hemp in addition, and all the different kinds of nuts. Ripe fruit as well as carrots and all sorts of greenstuff should also be offered. Further, fresh twigs for gnawing are necessary. Eggbread, rusks, and soaked crusty rolls or white bread are greatly liked. To help keep the plumage in good condition, the animal should be sprayed with water every so often.

The Grey Parrot has been bred in captivity on various occasions. The incubation period is 30 days, and the nestling stage lasts for about ten weeks.

The Grey Parrot lives in forest regions of tropical Africa. It is distributed from the west coast of Africa—the eastern Ivory Coast to as far as what used to be the Portuguese Congo—through the interior of the continent to Uganda, western Kenya, to the east coast of Lake Victoria and western Tanzania. Elsewhere in eastern Africa it does not occur. It is, however, found on the western African islands of

A trio of Black-winged Lovebirds. The male is the bird with the patch of red on its forehead.

Fernando Póo and Principe.

The nominate form *Psittacus erithacus erithacus*, i.e., the true Grey Parrot, is spread over what is by far the largest part of the range. In Guinea, Sierra Leone, Liberia, and probably in the western part of the Ivory Coast as well, the species is represented by *Psittacus erithacus timneh*, the Timneh Grey Parrot. This subspecies is slightly smaller, measuring 30 to 32 cm in length, and of a darker gray.

The two species of the genus *Coracopsis* are of an almost uniform brownish black coloration. They have a rather long, slightly rounded tail. The Black Parrot (*Coracopsis nigra*) is about 35 cm long, and its four races are found on Madagascar, the Comoro Islands, Grand Comore and Anjouan, and on the island of Praslin in the Seychelles. The Vasa Parrot (*Coracopsis vasa*) is much larger (50 cm). Its three races, too, are spread over Madagascar and the Comoro Islands, Mohéli, Grand Comore, and Anjouan. Parrots of the genus *Coracopsis* are a rarity on the bird market.

FAMILY PSITTACULIDAE

The family Psittaculidae is comprised of 53 species (this includes the four species of the genus *Psittacella* from New Guinea, whose place in this family is open to question). To these should be added several species that became extinct in more recent years. In many species of this family, the beak is wax red in color. Some birds are long-tailed, some have a short, rounded tail. In others, the truncated tail is straight at the tip. The majority of species are native to southern Asia, but the range of this family is extended westward to Africa by the genus *Agapornis* and one *Psittacula* species and, by a number of genera, eastward to as far as New Guinea, northeastern Australia, and the Solomon Islands.

A Vasa Parrot (the larger bird) and a Black Parrot. These species are relatively rare on the bird market.

Their closest relatives are the Polytelidae, and many authors do not in fact regard the latter as a separate group at all. It would appear, however, that the ancestors of the Polytelidae split away from the stem of the Psittaculidae at quite an early stage. If the Grey Parrots (family Psittacidae) have evolved from the Psittaculidae (i.e., via the genus *Mascarinus*, now extinct, and the genus *Coracopsis* from Madagascar) and not, as is frequently assumed, from Aratinginae ancestors, then that would be an additional reason for separating the Psittaculidae and the Polytelidae, since the former would then be much closer to the Grey Parrots (as far as stem history is concerned, not in characteristics) than to the Polytelidae, to which they bear a much greater resemblance.

Polytelidae: a family of slender, long-tailed parrots that are native to Australia, New Guinea, and several nearby islands, e.g. Alexandrine Parrot.

A colloquy of colorful Lovebirds, species *Agapornis*. Lovebirds got their name from their frequent mutual preening.

". . .[Lovebirds] not only delight with their appearance but are also extremely undemanding, require less space than other parrots because of their small size, are easy to breed, and, last but not least, are available at prices people can afford to pay."

A special position in the family, to some extent, is occupied by the genus *Agapornis*. On account of its not inconsiderable resemblance to the Hanging Parrots (genus *Loriculus)* and genera such as *Prioniturus* and *Bolbopsittacus*, which most certainly belong to the Psittaculidae, it is included, however.

The *Agapornis* species, popularly known as Lovebirds, are among the bird fanciers' greatest favorites, and this is hardly surprising. These small, short-tailed parrots (roughly the size of a sparrow) not only delight with their appearance but are also extremely undemanding, require less space than other parrots because of their small size, are easy to breed, and, last but not least, are available at prices people can afford to pay. What is more, some species are always on the market; the birds

offered for sale have been raised domestically. It would be wrong, however, not to describe the other side of the coin. It must be pointed out that many Lovebirds are rather quarrelsome, and some of them are downright malicious in the way they treat not only their own kind but also birds of other species. There are some awful screamers among them as well, and generally speaking they cannot be described as confiding birds, nor do they grow as tame as the other parrots. Their talent for talking does not amount to much, either.

The Lovebirds are native to Africa and (one species) to Madagascar. There is some disagreement among ornithologists as to how many species there are. Some assume there are nine species while others consider several of these to be only subspecies, thereby bringing the total number of species down to six or seven. Lovebirds nest inside hollow tree-trunks, inside termite mounds, and a few species transport the nest material (small wood shavings, leaves of grass, small pieces of bark they strip off branches) tucked away among the feathers on the lower region of the back. While some merely prepare a bed for the eggs, others construct domed nests. The clutch is generally comprised of three to five eggs which, on an average, are incubated for 20 to 21 days by most species. The young leave the nest at 30 days and the adult birds go on feeding them for a time. Once they have become independent, however, they must be separated from the adults, else squabbles will inevitably result, not to mention biting.

Lovebirds can be left in outdoor aviaries with a heated shelter during

"Lovebirds nest inside hollow tree-trunks, inside termite mounds, and a few species transport nest material. . .tucked away among the feathers on the lower region of the back."

The Black-collared Lovebird, a very rare Lovebird species, has a diet which primarily consists of wild figs. This makes the prospect of keeping it very difficult.

Steppe: terrain that is arid and contains vegetation that requires very little moisture, the soil in which is loamy and mostly deposited by the wind.

the winter months, but they should be allowed to keep their nestboxes for roosting and as protection when the nights are cold. It is preferable, however, to fetch them indoors for the winter. They can quickly be adapted to freely flying in and out. Since terrain with shrubs and trees constitutes their natural habitat, they are not as liable to run amok when startled as, for example, the Budgerigar, which, being a steppe-dweller, seeks to escape from danger by getting as far away as possible.

The Lovebirds hide themselves away in the nearest shrub or the top of the nearest tree and always remain within earshot of members of their own species. Unlike the Australian parrots, which hardly ever find their way back, they do not have a tendency to get lost. Losses are, therefore, very rare. Lovebirds make no special demands where their diet is concerned. They should be given millet, canary seed, oats, sunflower seeds, hemp (in small quantities), greenstuff, half-ripened seeds and

Artist's rendering of Red-faced Lovebirds. Red-faced Lovebirds are more delicate than most Lovebird species and are very difficult to breed, due to their unusual nesting habits.

fresh twigs for nibbling. For breeding birds, this diet is supplemented with ant pupae, grated yolk of hard-boiled egg, biscuits, rusks, and soaked white bread. In addition, one can offer a soft-food mix.

The basic color of the Lovebirds' plumage is a bright green in a variety of shades. Except for two species, where the female lacks the additional colors that characterize parts of the male's plumage, it is not possible to distinguish the sexes by the colors of their plumage. In some species, however, the females are noticeably bigger. Their broader pelvis also makes them perch with the feet further apart. It has been recorded that the distance between their feet is roughly 1 cm greater than in the males. Furthermore, the sexes can be differentiated by the difference in behavior. Sexing is difficult, however, for anyone who is unfamiliar with these birds.

The species that has still not been imported is the Black-collared Lovebird (*Agapornis swinderniana*). It has a length of 13 cm. Plumage is green, breast olive-yellow, a black ring around the neck, behind it a henna red ring (more or less distinct, depending on the subspecies); rump, upper tail coverts ultra navy blue; tail red at the root, with a black band below the green tip. Beak blackish. Three races are known. These are *Agapornis swinderniana swinderniana* from Liberia, *Agapornis swinderniana zenkeri* from Cameroon and Gabon, and, finally, *Agapornis swinderniana emini* from central Zaire to western Uganda. In its natural habitat, the Black-collared Lovebird feeds primarily on wild figs. This would need to be taken into consideration should the bird ever be imported.

Frequently imported is the Black-winged Lovebird (*Agapornis taranta*) from Ethiopia. There are two races: *Agapornis taranta taranta* and the

slightly smaller *Agapornis taranta nanus*. The sexes are easy to tell apart, as the female does not possess either a red forehead or red eyerings. The Black-winged Lovebird attains a length of 15.5 to 16.5 cm; the female is slightly smaller. These Lovebirds have frequently been bred in captivity. The species nests inside wooden boxes, into which it carries all sorts of nest materials in its neck and rump plumage (like the Red-faced Lovebird) and then lines the nest hollow with it. Breeding is as successful in a not-too-cramped cage as it is in the aviary. The clutch is comprised of three to four eggs, the incubation period spans a minimum of 24 days, and the young leave the nestbox at the age of about seven weeks. Black-winged Lovebirds are aggressive, particularly towards smaller and weaker birds, and have a tendency to savage the legs of their victims. Voice is a chattering song. According to Hampe, the call note is a thin and high-pitched "pseep psee-eep" or "prreep."

A male Grey-headed Lovebird. It is imperative that this species be given plenty of space.

Race: alternative name for subspecies, a taxonomical division which ranks below species, specifying that the members of different subspecies have some physical differences but can interbreed successfully, especially where their ranges overlap.

A pair of Masked Lovebirds. Masked Lovebirds have been known to fight with other Lovebirds, especially during the breeding season.

Nest hollow: the interior of the nestbox where the nest is built.

The Red-faced Lovebird (*Agapornis pullaria*) was imported very frequently in the past. There are two races, with a range that extends from western Africa (northern Angola to the Gold Coast) eastward to as far as southwestern Ethiopia and the Lake Victoria region. The species has a length of 13 to 15 cm. The female is slightly paler all over and the face is more yellowish red.

The Red-faced Lovebird is a bit delicate at first and needs to be acclimatized carefully. It is a quiet bird and usually a peaceable one. Breeding it in captivity is not quite as easy as it is with other Lovebirds and, so far, fully successful attempts have remained rare. According to H. Hampe, the reason for this must be sought in its nesting habits, which differ from those of other Lovebirds. In its natural habitat, the Red-faced Lovebird breeds inside the nests of tree-dwelling termites and ants, which explains its reluctance to use the wooden nestboxes that are normally offered to birds in captivity. H. Hampe experimented with mud heaps as a substitute for the mounds constructed by termites but was not completely successful. Thick chunks of cork have also been tried out as a substitute, but again the result was not convincing. Breeding inside ordinary nestboxes has nonetheless been accomplished on several occasions.

The nest hollow is lined with a thin layer of willow leaves and pieces of bark, all chewed into small fragments and carried in by the female, tucked away among the feathers on the rump or almost anywhere else she can reach with the beak. The clutch consists of three to five eggs. These are incubated by the female alone for a period of 21 days. The Red-faced Lovebird has a pleasant voice.

A species that in the past was always readily available but which has hardly been offered for sale since the export embargo was imposed on Madagascan birds is the Grey-headed Lovebird (*Agapornis cana*) from Madagascar. There are two races, namely *Agapornis cana cana*, which occurs in the north of the island, and *Agapornis cana ablectanea*, found in the southwest. The Grey-headed Lovebird has become naturalized on the islands of Mauritius, Réunion, and Rodriguez, and on the Comoro Islands and the Seychelles. It attains a length of 13 to 14 cm. The female is distinguished from the male by having green feathers on the head and breast instead of pearl gray ones.

Grey-headed Lovebirds are extraordinarily shy and anxious and get used to the keeper very slowly, if at all. I do not have any pleasant memories of them. There was not one bird among the several pairs of Grey-headed Lovebirds I owned over the years that grew tame or confiding. Usually when I approached their cages, they disappeared inside the nestbox amidst loud screams and did not show themselves again for a long time. Despite their shyness, all the pairs got down to breeding, however, and a few chicks hatched, although not a single one fledged.

"Grey-headed Lovebirds are extraordinarily shy and anxious and get used to the keeper very slowly, if at all."

Peach-faced Lovebirds come in a wide spectrum of colors.

The young invariably died during the developmental stage. Why I cannot say. Hampe, in his book *The Lovebirds,* also writes, "Breeding does not always proceed quite smoothly and the success rate is not exactly high." The well-known amateur ornithologist H. Lauer, writes, "After years of experience, I have to say that the Grey-headed Lovebirds breed very unreliably and one has to expect many unpleasant incidents." Other breeders report better results, and one even goes so far as to say, "Sometimes they breed prolifically." What is important is to let a pair of Grey-headed Lovebirds have plenty of space, which is necessary for breeding and is fiercely defended against intruders.

The nest is constructed, inside the usual Budgerigar box, from bits of bark and leaf fragments (willow leaves are preferred) which the female carries into the box in the back and rump plumage. The clutch generally consists of four eggs which are incubated for about 21 days. The young leave the nestbox at the age of about five weeks. Once they have become independent, it is prudent to separate them from the parents, especially where these are starting another brood.

There are occasional imports of the Peach-faced Lovebird (*Agapornis*

Developmental stage: the time period that begins when the young are hatched and ends when they are fully fledged.

A pair of Nyasa Lovebirds. Most Lovebirds enjoy having a nestbox for roosting when kept in a heated outdoor aviary.

Fischer's
Lovebirds.
Note the large
white eyerings
on these birds.

Fischer's Lovebirds are quite common on the bird market, as they are relatively good breeders and are very attractive birds.

Naturalized: when a race or species not native to an area is introduced, becomes acclimatized, and makes this area its new habitat.

roseicollis), the nominate form of which, *Agapornis roseicollis roseicollis*, lives in southern Angola, while the subspecies *Agapornis roseicollis catumbella* occurs in the coastal region of central Angola. Its length of 16 to 17.5 cm makes the Peach-faced the largest Lovebird. As opposed to the Grey-headed, the Peach-faced can be described as bold. It does not grow confiding, however, and becomes tame very rarely and only if kept on its own. Its shrill, piercing screams can be an extreme nuisance. In association with other birds, the Peach-faced Lovebird is ill-natured. For this reason, it can only be kept with larger species, but even then caution is necessary since Peach-faced Lovebirds have a tendency to chew up the legs of their fellow inmates.

Breeding the species presents no problems. The female carries the nest material into the box in the plumage of the lower back and rump and builds a roofed nest. The clutch comprises three to five eggs; the incubation period is 21 to 22 days, and the young leave the nest at the age of about five weeks. In the natural environment of the Peach-faced Lovebird, a blue variety has been observed.

The group of four Lovebirds that will be described next differ from the species that have been dealt with so far not only by having broad white eyerings but also on account of transporting the nest material in the beak instead of the plumage. There is no agreement among authors on the birds' taxonomic arrangement. Despite the great differences in coloration, some authors regard them all as subspecies of one single species which is called *Agapornis personata* (Masked Lovebird). Others maintain that each form is a species in its own right, while a third school of thought combines the Nyasa Lovebird and the Black-cheeked Lovebird into the species *Agapornis lilianae* but ascribes independent status to the two remaining forms. Here, albeit with some reservation, all forms are treated as species.

The Masked Lovebird (*Agapornis personata*) is found in central Tanzania from Lake Manyara to Lake Rukwa. On the coast near Dar es Salaam it has become naturalized. It grows to a length of about 15 to 16 cm. The female is slightly bigger than the male and her head is more blackish brown in color.

The Masked Lovebird is comparatively easy to breed, but the

Peach-faced lovebird. These birds are noisy and gregarious in the wild.

pair should be kept on its own—i.e., not together with other Lovebirds—if at all possible. Breeding is also likely to succeed in the cage, which should be at least 80 cm long. The nestbox should have a clear width of about 12 to 14 cm and a height of 25 cm. For the entrance hole a width of about 4 to 5 cm is recommended. The average clutch consists of three to five eggs, and these are incubated for 21 days. The young fledge at the approximate age of 35 days.

Unfortunately, the Masked has frequently been crossed with other forms of Lovebirds, and what one sees in pet shops and fanciers' aviaries are often undefinable hybrids. The latter never come anywhere near the genuine beauty of the pure Masked Lovebird. In fact, what all these hybrids have in common, to a greater or lesser degree, is a faded appearance of the color of the head. As must be expected when a bird is bred often, sooner or later there will be color mutations. Thus not only blue mutations have appeared but also yellow and white ones. Generally speaking, the purity of these colors still leaves a lot to be desired, however. Furthermore, a proportion of these animals are the products of mass-breeding establishments and have little vitality.

Probably the best known of all Lovebirds is Fischer's Lovebird (*Agapornis fischeri*). It hails from part of Tanzania, i.e., the area south and southeast of Lake Victoria. It has a length of 14 to 15 cm. The female's plumage is identical to the male's, but, like all females of the four Lovebirds with white eyerings, she is larger than the male. This does not mean, however, that the sexes are easy to differentiate. This form, too, breeds readily and at times quite prolifically under the conditions described above. A yellow mutation occurred in the '30s but disappeared again, and the number of yellow

Fischer's Lovebirds. In the Lovebird species with white eyerings, the female bird is larger than the male.

Color mutations: variations which can occur in the wild, albeit rarely (as they are more likely to attract the attention of predators than normally colored birds), but are most often selectively bred for by man.

Heterozygous: the genetic state of an animal which, in parrots, implies that it is not a pure member of a race or species.

birds is still very small. With their red head and plumage of pure yellow, these individuals look very attractive. Incidentally, these yellow Fischer's Lovebirds are said to be good breeders.

A further species is the Nyasa Lovebird (*Agapornis lilianae*), from western Malawi, eastern Zambia, and the lower Zambezi valley. It grows to a length of 13 to 14 cm. Fr. V. Lucanus describes a hand-reared Nyasa Lovebird which, in a slightly hard and hissing voice, was able to say the words, "Come here, where are you"—a considerable achievement for one of the Lovebirds, whose ability to talk is not great as a rule.

There are no special points to make as regards breeding. By and large, what has been said about the earlier forms in that respect also applies here. A few years ago a

yellow mutation occurred in Holland, but nothing more has ever been heard about these animals with red markings on the head and a basically yellow plumage. At more or less the same time, a report appeared in Denmark on a stock of yellow Nyasa Lovebirds. With the exception of one heterozygous hen, however, the entire stock was destroyed by disease.

The fourth Lovebird with white eyerings is the Black-cheeked Lovebird (*Agapornis nigrigenis*). It occurs in southwestern Zambia, i.e., on the northern tributaries of the Zambezi between Sesheke, and the Victoria Falls, and in the eastern part of the Caprivi Strip of Namibia. It measures 14 to 15.3 cm in length. Black-cheeked Lovebirds breed readily and reliably. They grow more confiding than other Lovebirds and can be recommended

A male Blue-crowned Hanging Parrot. This species is the best known of the Hanging Parrots. These birds feed on berries, fruit, and flower nectar.

particularly to the novice, all the more so since their behavior is more peaceable, on the whole, towards other kinds of birds as well.

Similar to the Lovebirds in many respects are the Hanging Parrots (genus *Loriculus*), which grow to a length of about 11 to 16 cm and are distributed over New Guinea, the Maluku Islands, the Sunda Islands, the Philippines, India, and Sri Lanka. These birds owe their name to their peculiar habit of hanging upside-down from the branches like bats. They not only rest in this position but also maintain it when feeding. They are frugivorous and feed on flower nectar, berries, and fruit. A consequence of their diet is that their feces are very liquid. The latter get sprayed a long way. Hanging Parrots are extraordinarily beautiful, lively, and active small birds. They are harmless and peaceable, although often engaging in squabbles with members of their own species. They are very nimble climbers. Like some of the Lovebirds, they transport the nest material between the feathers of the lower back, the breast, and the shoulder region.

In the past, some of the 11 species of Hanging Parrots were imported in fairly large numbers. Unfortunately, they often arrive in a less than satisfactory condition, apparently due to the wrong kind of diet, and therefore need to be acclimatized very carefully. They should be offered all kinds of fruit, a good soft-food, eggbread, rusk, ant pupae, whatever greenstuff is available, a variety of smallish seeds such as millet (including sprays), and canary seed.

The cage that is to accommodate Hanging Parrots must be equipped with branches on the ceiling so that the birds are able to not only climb but can also hang upside-down as is their habit. A few species have been bred in captivity with good results.

The voice of the Hanging Parrot is an eager, softly singing chatter.

The best known of these birds is the Blue-crowned Hanging Parrot (*Loriculus galgulus*), which is native to Malacca, Sumatra, the Anambas Islands, Nias, Riau, and the islands of Bangka, Belitung, Borneo, the Labuan and Maratua Islands, and Enggano Island.

The Blue-crowned Hanging Parrot grows to a length of about 13 cm. The female lacks the blue spot on the crown and the red spot on the throat. The Blue-crowned has been bred in captivity. An ordinary Budgerigar nestbox constitutes a suitable nesting facility. The female carries the nest material (small twigs or pieces of stripped bark) between the rump feathers.

A species that is being imported less frequently is the larger (length 15 cm) Philippine Hanging Parrot (*Loriculus philippensis*). Numerous subspecies exist, all occurring on the Philippines. Plumage is green, forehead red, a golden yellow spot on the nape; rump red with blue

Black-cheeked Lovebirds are less quarrelsome than other Lovebirds, and they also become more confiding.

"[Hanging Parrots] owe their name to their peculiar habit of hanging upside-down from the branches like bats."

83

A male Philippine Hanging Parrot. The quarters of all Hanging Parrots should be furnished with branches hung from the ceiling, so that the birds are able to hang upside-down.

Indochina: southeast Asian peninsula which includes Burma, Cambodia, Laos, Thailand, Vietnam, and the Malay peninsula.

A trio of Plum-headed Parakeets. These birds come from India and Sri Lanka.

sides, upper tail coverts red, a large red spot on the throat, cheeks green, underside green, beak orange-red. In the female, the cheeks are blue and the red spot on the throat is absent.

Another species which is rarely available on the market is the Vernal Hanging Parrot *(Loriculus vernalis)*. Its range extends from southern India via Bangladesh to Thailand and Indochina and also includes the Andaman Islands. The bird grows to 16.7 cm in length. Plumage is green, males with a light blue spot on the throat; rump, upper tail coverts brownish, tail feathers light blue below, beak red.

On the Philippines, Celebes, and Buru (Moluccas) live the six species of the genus *Prioniturus*, among them the Blue-crowned Racket-

tailed Parrot (*Prioniturus discurus*), a bird with a blue crown, otherwise mainly green above, yellowish green below. The tail is truncated, straight at the end; the two median feathers are elongated, their shafts bare; only the tip of the feather bears a vane. The tail is similar in structure in the other species of this genus. The five races of the Blue-crowned Racket-tailed Parrot are distributed over the Philippines. The species has a length of about 27 cm.

Also native to the Philippines are the four races of the Guaiabero (*Bolbopsittacus lunulatus*), a species which in size and build resembles a thick-billed Lovebird. Plumage is mainly green, with blue on the forehead, in the eye region, on the anterior portion of the cheeks, and on the throat; a blue band around the neck and a greenish yellow rump. The tail is very short, the powerful beak gray in color. Length is 15 cm.

Parrots of the genus *Eclectus* are rather stately animals (length 35 to 40 cm) with a powerful bill, a short tail, and a pronounced difference in

coloration between the sexes. The genus is comprised of a single species, *Eclectus roratus*, the Eclectus Parrot. There are approximately ten races. Their range extends from the Lesser Sunda Islands via New Guinea to the Solomon Islands and northeastern Australia. One of the best known subspecies is *Eclectus roratus polychloros*, the New Guinea Eclectus Parrot. What is particularly interesting, where the Eclectus Parrots are concerned, is that the sexes are not only completely different in color but that the female is the more brightly colored of the two while the male is green. It is hardly surprising that it was once thought that there were red species and green species of this genus, until thorough research showed that the green and red Eclectus Parrots belong together as males and females.

They are calm, quiet birds which quickly grow tame and learn to talk as well. They are rather delicate, however, and, despite the magnificent color of the plumage cannot, because of their serious

A female Eclectus Parrot. It is very unusual for the female of a species to be more brightly colored than the male.

"[Eclectus Parrots] are calm, quiet birds which quickly grow tame and learn to talk as well."

A yellow mutation of the Moustached Parakeet.

A pair of Derbyan Parakeets, a male and a female. The male has the bright red beak.

Alexander the Great: Macedonian king who was born in 356 BC and ruled from 336 to 323 BC, known for his conquest of Persia and his travels through India.

personality which is quite alien to all other parrots, be greatly recommended as pets. In addition to the usual seeds, they need to be given small quantities of fruit on a regular basis, and berries and biscuits. Fresh branches, especially from conifers, must be at their disposal at all times. Eclectus Parrots have been successfully bred in captivity on several occasions.

Parakeets of the genus *Psittacula* were brought back to Europe from India in 330 B.C. by the commander-in-chief of the navy of Alexander the Great, hence the popular name Alexandrine Parakeet for one of the species. All these parrots are of medium size and of a powerful but slender build. They have a long tail, with the feathers arranged in steps; the two median tail feathers are elongated. There are 13 surviving species; three others became extinct relatively recently. Members of the genus are found predominantly in Asia, in India, on Sri Lanka and the Sunda Islands, and in southern China. A single species from India also occurs in Africa. Birds of this genus have been widely kept since ancient times. They are hardy but often shy, liable to bite, quarrelsome, bad screamers, and, above all, they do a lot of damage to wood. Given the right treatment, however, young animals in particular grow tame; a few species have shown themselves to be quite talented talkers. Not just because of their size but above all because of their liveliness, they should be kept only in spacious cages or, better still, aviaries. All species have been successfully bred in captivity.

The diet consists of a good variety of seeds such as millet, canary seed, oats, sunflower seeds, rice (complete with husks), hemp, maize (the latter also in a soaked condition), nuts of all kinds, and fruit and plenty of greenstuff. Fresh branches for gnawing should not be lacking. The birds also require a supplement in the form of a soft-food mix. Ant pupae and mealworms are given, too, as are eggbread, white bread or rusks, and, finally, both cereals and grass seeds in a semi-mature state. Many species can safely be left in outdoor aviaries with an enclosed shelter during the winter months.

The Moustached Parakeet

(*Psittacula alexandri*) is found in the Himalayan range. From there, its distribution extends to southern China and Indochina, the Andaman Islands, the islands to the west of Sumatra, Java, Bali, and Kangean. It grows to a length of about 33.5 to 35 cm. The basic color of the plumage is green, as in the parrots described earlier. The head is gray with a tinge of blue. A narrow black edging runs from under the lower mandible around the cheeks. Crop and breast pink, an olive-yellow patch on the wings. Beak red or wholly or partially black, depending on the species. Eyes light yellow, feet grayish brown.

There are eight subspecies of the Moustached Parakeet. Only one shall be mentioned here in more detail, however—*Psittacula alexandri fasciata*, which periodically appears on the market in fairly large numbers. This parakeet has a length of 35 to 40 cm; the tail is about 20

Mealworms: larvae of Tenebrionidid beetles which often infest grains, used for bait in fishing and as food for insectivores.

Fruit and greenstuff are important supplements to the diet of the Plum-headed Parakeet.

Headstudy of a male Alexandrine Parakeet. Once tame, this bird may be kept on a stand and has the potential to become a good talker.

Genus: taxonomical rank, between family and species, based on evolutionary similarities between related species; a unique species with isolated characteristics can also be given its own genus within its particular family.

cm long. In this bird the rose color of the breast is quite dark, with a tinge of lilac, and very extensive. The beak is red above, black below, black all over in the female. The color of the beak alone makes this race easy to differentiate from *Psittacula alexandri alexandri* with its completely red beak. Distribution is from the Himalayan range to northern India, Haiman and southern China. This parakeet can grow tame and learn to talk. Like many of its closest relatives, however, it screams unpleasantly.

With a length of 54 cm, Blyth's Parakeet (*Psittacula caniceps*), from the Nicobar Islands, is the largest member of the genus. It is only mentioned here for the sake of completeness. Imports have always been few and far between.

The Derbyan Parakeet (*Psittacula derbiana*), only very seldom imported, looks very similar to the Moustached Parakeet but, measuring 40 to 50 cm in length, is considerably larger. It is native to southeastern Tibet and southwestern China. Its range extends further north than that of any other parrot. In the male the upper mandible is red, the lower mandible black. The female's beak is completely black. In the Derbyan Parakeet the head is gray-blue, with a black band on the forehead. The lores and a broad stripe below the sides of the head are also black. The upper part of the back of the head and the ear coverts are lilac-blue, the sides of the neck and the breast bluish violet. As in its relatives already mentioned, the basic color is green. The Derbyan Parakeet is not as active as the other representatives of the group.

Now to the Alexandrine Parakeet (*Psittacula eupatria*), an extremely beautiful bird with a total length of 45 to 50 cm. The length of the tail is about 28 cm. The five races are widespread in India to as far as Indochina. The plumage is grass green, with a grayish blue hue on the back of the head and the cheeks. A black line extends from the nostrils to the eyes. The cheeks and sides of the head are bordered by a black band. There is a rose collar around the neck and a maroon patch on the shoulders. The beak is red, the eyes are whitish yellow, the feet pale gray or lead gray. In the female, the collar and the black edging around the cheeks are absent. Being a tame bird and a good talker, the Alexandrine Parakeet is also kept free on a stand. Breeding presents no problems. The nestbox should have an internal base of about 30 by 30 cm and a clear height of 50 cm. Breeding in captivity has already resulted in blue and lutino mutations. As early as 1926 an illustration in color in the *Avicultural Magazine* showed a wild blue Alexandrine that had been taken out of the nest in the species' natural habitat.

The range of the Alexandrine Parakeet extends from Sri Lanka and the Indian subcontinent to Indochina. It also occurs on the Andaman Islands. The nominate form, *Psittacula eupatria eupatria*, is found in southern India and Sri Lanka. In northern and central India the species is represented by *Psittacula eupatria nipalensis*, which, with a total length of 50 to 52 cm, is slightly larger, as well as being more greenish blue-gray on the head.

The subspecies *Psittacula eupatria avensis*, found in Kachin and Burma, southward to as far as Amherst, has a weaker bill. Thailand, Laos, Cambodia, and Vietnam constitute the natural range of *Psittacula euptria siamensis*. The race *Psittacula eupatria magnirostis* hails from the Andaman Islands. As its name implies, it has a stronger bill. Another differential characteristic is

Lutino: a mutation in which melanin is not produced, usually resulting in a yellowish bird; lutino is always recessive.

A male Rose-ringed Parakeet. This species is particularly known for its incessant destruction of wood. If provided with enough chewing material, however, it can become a good pet.

The Plum-headed Parakeet has a pleasant song and is not known for screaming, as are some closely related species.

Taxonomy: the study and classification of plants and animals according to natural evolutionary relationships.

The Alexandrine Parakeet got its name from Alexander the Great, as parrots from this genus were brought to Europe by one of his naval officers circa 330 BC.

a lighter patch on the wings.

A very closely related species, the Seychelles Parakeet (*Psittacula wardi*), occurred on the Seychelles until it became extinct towards the end of the 19th century. By some taxonomists this parakeet was regarded as merely a subspecies of the Alexandrine.

One species of the genus *Psittacula* is native to southern Asia, from India and Sri Lanka to Burma. In addition, two of its races are found in the northernmost part of tropical Africa, from southern Mauritania and Senegal in the west to Ethiopia and northern Somalia in the east. This is the Rose-ringed Parakeet (*Psittacula krameri*). In many areas it was introduced by man, on Zanzibar, in parts of Kenya, Egypt, Saudi Arabia, Iraq, Afghanistan, and

southern China, and on the island of Mauritius—already the home of a closely related and very similar species which, however, differs in behavior, the Mauritius Parakeet (*Psittacula echo*), which is now extremely rare. The latter is confined to remote forest regions, whereas the Rose-ringed Parakeet occurs on cultivated land. It must be pointed out, however, that the female lacks the black stripe on the cheeks and the rose-colored collar. Although this Parakeet is comparatively easy to tame, can learn to talk, and even utters a pleasant song, the reader must be warned about its shrill, piercing, and deafening screams. It can also be rather ill-natured, and when it comes to destroying wood, this species is just about the worst offender of the whole group. Because of its beauty it is a favorite nonetheless, and breeding it presents no problem either. The nestbox should have a clear width of about 20 by 20 cm and a height of 30 cm. The entrance hole should measure 8 cm in diameter. Lutinos and blue mutations have already been produced of this species, too.

The Rose-ringed Parakeets on the bird market generally originate from India and belong to the subspecies *Psittacula krameri manillensis,* from southern India and Sri Lanka, and *Psittacula krameri borealis* from northern India and Burma. The African races consist of *Psittacula krameri krameri* from the western part of the range, i.e., from southern Mauritania, Senegal, and Guinea to the Nile and western Uganda, and *Psittacula krameri parvirostris* from northeast Africa, i.e., from eastern Sudan and northern Ethiopia to northern Somalia. The Rose-ringed Parakeet attains a total length of 40 to 42.5 cm; the tail is about 24 cm long.

A particularly handsome and charming representative of this

genus is the Plum-headed Parakeet (*Psittacula cyanocephala*) from India and Sri Lanka. It has a total length of 37 cm; the tail measures 20 to 22.5 cm. This parakeet does not scream. In fact, it has a rather pleasant voice and utters its song particularly during the breeding season. It is a peaceable bird as a rule and, in a larger flight cage or in the aviary, can be kept in association with smaller birds, too, even waxbills. Young Plum-headed Parakeets raised in captivity quickly grow tame and can be trained. Some individuals show an ability for talking. The diet should consist of a normal seed-mix, i.e., various kinds of millet, canary seed, hulled oats, wheat, a small quantity of hemp, sunflower seeds, and grass and oat seeds in a half-ripe condition. Soft-food is essential, particularly where young birds are being raised. Fruit and greenstuff should not be absent, and fresh branches should be provided for gnawing.

Breeding presents no difficulty. The nestbox, with an area of about 18 by 18 cm, a height of about 30 cm

A pair of Blossom-headed Parakeets. This species is very similar to the Plum-headed Parakeet.

"...[The Plum-headed Parakeet] has a rather pleasant voice and utters its song particularly during the breeding season."

The Slaty-headed Parakeet is rarely imported and is not often found on the bird market today.

Temperate: the climate of the regions located between the Tropic of Cancer and the arctic circle in the northern hemisphere or between the Tropic of Capricorn and the antarctic circle in the southern hemisphere.

(internal dimensions), and an entrance hole measuring about 6 cm in diameter, should be lined with a layer of sawdust inside the nest hollow. The incubation period spans 21 to 23 days, and the young leave the nestbox at the age of 42 days. The head of the young birds is greenish gray or ash gray in color. They thus resemble the female, which has a blue-gray head, not a plum-colored one like the male. The hen also lacks the maroon spot on the shoulders. Although Plum-headed Parakeets can be left in outdoor aviaries with temperate shelters during the winter months, they undoubtedly feel more comfortable in heated rooms. The only mutation that has been heard of so far consists of lutinos.

Whereas in northern India and Bengal the Plum-headed Parakeet is represented by the slightly larger subspecies *Psittacula cyanocephala bengalensis*, it occurs in the nominate form *Psittacula cyanocephala cyanocephala* in southern India and Sri Lanka. A closely related species, the Blossom-headed Parakeet (*Psittacula roseata*), is found from Bengal and Assam to Indochina. The coloration of its plumage is very like that of its cousin, except that in this species the head is rose-colored and the maroon spot on the shoulders is

Superb Parrot. The migration of this species in the wild seems to coincide with the flowering of eucalyptus plants.

Shoulders: the areas where the wings join the body.

present in both sexes. The Blossom-headed Parakeet is imported less frequently. In behavior, etc., it is identical to its cousin and, like the latter, it has already been bred in captivity. Hybrids have been produced by crossing the Blossom-headed with the Plum-headed Parakeet.

A species which very seldom appears on the bird market is the Slaty-headed Parakeet (*Psittacula himalayana*). It occurs from northern India to western Assam, breeds at altitudes of up to 2600 m and more, and descends to areas between 700 and 1300 m in the winter. This parakeet has a length of about 40 cm, and the tail is 23 cm long. The basic color of the plumage is green. The head is blackish slate gray. There is a black band on the chin, nape of a light bluish green color. A small maroon spot on the shoulders is absent in the female. Eyes straw yellow, beak red, lower mandible paler, feet grayish green.

Very closely related to the Slaty-headed Parakeet, perhaps even a race of the latter, is Hume's Parakeet (*Psittacula finschii*). It has a lighter, more bluish head, its basic color is more yellowish green and the beak more orange-red. It occurs in eastern Assam, southwestern China, Tenasserim, northern Thailand,

A Malabar Parakeet. This species must be carefully acclimatized. It is usually not as active as other members of its genus.

southern Laos, and central Annam. With a length of 41 cm, it is slightly larger than the Slaty-headed Parakeet.

There are occasional imports of the Malabar Parakeet (*Psittacula columboides*), which is native to southwestern India. It grows to a total length of 36 to 39 cm, the tail reaches 24 cm. Head, neck, upper back, breast, gray; a blue band on the forehead; lores, eyerings green; below the sides of the head, across the nape, a black and bluish green band which grows broader on the throat. The rest of the plumage bluish green, rump light blue, the median tail feathers blue, green along the edge and yellow at the tip. The upper mandible is red, with a horn white tip, the lower mandible reddish black. The female, which is smaller, is pale green on the neck, upper back, and breast, with a blackish beak. Like the Plum-headed Parakeet, this species is somewhat delicate at first and therefore needs special care in the early stages. Unlike the former, however, it is less active and, in fact,

rather lethargic. Neunzig writes: "Tend to sit motionless, only get off the perch to feed and drink; move awkwardly; bite all birds that come near them, although not attacking any birds in other circumstances." It is not clear whether this rather discouraging criticism was based on observations of cage or of aviary birds. This is not an unimportant point since, generally speaking, birds in the cage show a very different behavior from that exhibited in a larger flight room where they have plenty of space—often so different as to be unrecognizable. The voice of the Malabar Parakeet is not unpleasant.

On Sri Lanka the Malabar Parakeet is replaced by the Emerald-collared Parakeet (*Psittacula calthorpae*). The latter is much smaller, however (length about 29 cm).

From time to time there are imports of *Psittacula longicauda nicobaria*, which occurs on the Nicobar Islands. This is one of the five subspecies of the Long-tailed Parakeet (*Psittacula longicauda*). In

A male Superb Parrot. This bird is best kept in a spacious aviary.

Eyering: the bare area surrounding the eye, often called periophthalmic region.

A pair of Princess Parrots.

Opposite: Artist's rendering of an Amboina King Parrot, a species that is rarely found on the market. *Above, left:* A pair of lutino Rose-ringed Parakeets. *Above, right:* A male Eclectus Parrot. *Below:* A Long-tailed Parakeet. It has been reported that this species is very lethargic. It must be remembered, however, that behavior in captivity may differ from behavior in the wild.

Moustachial stripe: a dark band that runs from under the lower mandible around the cheeks.

Male (green) and female (red) Eclectus Parrots. For many years aviculturists did not realize that these complementary birds were members of the same species.

addition to the Nicobar Islands, the range of this species covers the Andaman Islands, Malaya, Sumatra and Borneo and some of the islands in their proximity. This parakeet attains a length of 40 cm. The overall color of the plumage is green, the crown is of a dull reddish color, the forehead dark bluish green, lores and broad moustachial stripe black, cheeks and ear coverts red. Primaries blue along the outer edge, likewise the primary coverts. Upper mandible red, lower mandible black; eyes yellow, feet grayish brown.

The true Long-tailed Parakeet, or the nominate form, *Psittacula longicauda longicauda*, which occurs on the Malayan peninsula (where its

range starts to the south of Perak), on Sumatra, Nias, Bangka, Belitung, the Anambas, and on Borneo, grows to a length of 40 cm, of which the tail makes up 22 to 25 cm. As in all parakeets of the group, the overall color of the plumage is green. The back and sides of the head are red, the moustachial stripe is black, rump and lower back light blue, wings blue; tail feathers green, median ones blue; eyes yellow; beak red above, black below; feet grayish brown. In the female the whole beak is black and the band below the cheeks is green, not black. Long-tailed Parakeets extremely rarely come on the market. According to Neunzig, they are lethargic and

quiet birds which mostly just sit about without moving.

The remaining races of the species *Psittacula longicauda* are *Psittacula longicauda tytleri* from the Andaman Islands, *Psittacula longicauda defontainei* from the Natuna Islands and other islands between Sumatra and Borneo, and *Psittacula longicauda modesta* from the island of Enggano. None of these races are ever seen on the market.

FAMILY POLYTELIDAE

This family, which is comprised of a mere ten species and in some respects forms a link between the Psittaculidae and the Loriidae and Platycercidae, includes a few of the most sought after and most highly valued species of parrots. Members of this family are slender parrots, mostly long-tailed (*Aprosmictus* being the exception), that are native to Australia, New Guinea, Timor and Wetar, the Moluccas, and the Fiji Islands.

The genus *Polytelis* consists of only one species. The latter has a long tail with a step-like arrangement of the feathers. Its home is Australia.

Restricted to a small range in the southeast Australian interior (northern Victoria and central New South Wales) is the Superb Parrot (*Polytelis swainsonii*), which has a length of 40 cm. The basic color of the plumage is green. The male has an orange forehead, yellow cheeks and throat, and a light red spot on the throat, whereas the female is green all over. The beak is red, the eyes are orange-yellow. The Superb Parrot is a fairly active bird and, unfortunately, a loud one as well, with a shrill, penetrating voice. It has repeatedly been bred in captivity with good results, particularly in spacious aviaries, inside which its personality comes much more into its own.

Closely related is the genus

Female Eclectus Parrot. The plumage of this species is so fine that it resembles fur.

A male Australian King Parrot. Australian King Parrots are occasionally available on the bird market, but they are generally an expensive acquisition.

Spathopterus with its two species. The Princess Parrot or Queen Alexandra's Parakeet *(Spathopterus alexandrae)* is very rare and consequently very expensive, too. It is distributed from the southern part of the Northern Territory and southwest Queensland to the northern part of South Australia, as well as occurring in the eastern part of Western Australia. Forehead and crown of a delicate light blue; cheeks, chin, and throat rose-colored; remaining plumage of the head, as well as the neck, back, and shoulders, olive brown-green; lower back and rump blue; upper tail coverts olive green, faded blue; underside gray-yellow; thighs rose-colored; wing coverts light yellow-green; eyes orange-yellow, red eyerings which are absent in the female; beak coral-red, feet brownish. Length is about 45 cm. This parakeet, too—an extraordinarily elegant, very long-tailed bird—needs ample flying space, all the more so on account of its liveliness. Its peaceble nature is worthy of note and means it can also

"*The Regent Parrot is a pleasant, confiding bird, and a peaceable one. Furthermore, it is hardy and can be left outdoors in the winter, assuming this agile flier has a very spacious aviary at its disposal.*"

be kept in association with smaller birds. There have been several successful breeding attempts in captivity. Unfortunately, this parrot has a loud voice, of which it often makes persistent use, and this can turn it into a real nuisance.

The second species of the genus *Spathopterus* is the Regent Parrot, one race of which occurs in southwestern Australia, the other in the interior of southeastern Australia (northwestern Victoria, southwestern New South Wales, the southeastern part of South Australia). Male plumage: head, neck, rump, upper tail coverts, underside bright yellow; head, neck, upper tail coverts faded olive; back olive yellow-green, lesser and median coverts yellow; greater coverts, shoulders, and wings black; tail black with a bluish sheen; eyes red, beak red with whitish gray ceres, feet blackish brown. Length 40 cm. The female is not as brightly colored—the overall effect is more olive green. The Regent Parrot is a pleasant, confiding bird, and a peaceable one. Furthermore, it is hardy and can be left outdoors in the winter, assuming this agile flier has a very spacious aviary at its disposal. It has repeatedly been bred with good results. Raising-food consists of germinated millet, especially spray millet, as well as other seeds in a half-ripe condition, sunflower seeds, dandelion, shepherd's purse, ragwort, oats (complete with ears), and half-ripe corn on the cob. A suitable (broad) nestbox should have a length of 40 cm, a depth of 28 cm, and a height of 25 cm. The incubation period spans 21 days.

The genus *Alisterus* (King Parrots) consists of three species, each with several races. The Australian King Parrot *(Alisterus scapularis)* is imported comparatively frequently. It occurs in the coastal regions and the adjoining hilly country of eastern and southeastern Australia from

A pair of Red-capped Parrots.

Nominative form: the trinomial scientific name of a subspecies in which the specific and subspecific names are the same, indicating that this was the first race of a species to be identified.

central Queensland through New South Wales to Victoria. In the northern part of this range it is represented by the subspecies *Alisterus scapularis minor,* in the southern part by the nominate form, *Alisterus scapularis scapularis.* The species has an approximate length of 37 to 40 cm, the tail measures 18 to 21 cm. The coloration of the male plumage is as follows: head, underside scarlet; a blue band on the nape; rump, upper tail coverts blue; back green; edge of wing, anterior wing coverts blue; tail black; under tail coverts scarlet, dark blue in the base; beak red, eyes yellow, feet dark gray. The female, on the other hand, shows the following coloration: head, nape, back, and wings are green; lower back and rump blue; belly scarlet; under tail coverts green with scarlet tips; throat and breast olive green, faded red; median tail

A male Regent Parrot. This species is peaceful and easy to breed. It does best in a roomy aviary, and it should be given a sufficiently large nestbox.

feathers green, beak reddish black. The Australian King Parrot is without a doubt one of the most beautiful of all the parrots, hence highly sought after but too expensive for many hobbyists. It also grows quite tame and is a quiet and peaceable bird. Like the preceding species, however, it must be kept in a very spacious aviary, where it can also be left in the winter, provided the outdoor flight is in a sheltered position. Breeding attempts in captivity have repeatedly been successful.

Another species is the Amboina King Parrot (*Alisterus amboinensis*), which resembles the Australian King Parrot and is native to the Moluccas, northwestern New Guinea and the neighboring islands. What distinguishes it from the Australian King Parrot, mainly, is that the red on the head and underside is more crimson. So far it has very seldom been imported and is just mentioned here for the sake of completeness. There are six subspecies. I have not heard of any breeding attempts in captivity.

Like the previous genus, the two species of the genus *Aprosmictus* come from Australia. They are, however, also found on New Guinea and the Lesser Sunda Islands (Timor and Wetar). They are distinguished by a shorter tail, the eight median feathers which are of equal length.

In the last few years the Red-winged Parrot (*Aprosmictus erythropterus*) has been imported on numerous occasions. The native range of the nominate form, *Aprosmictus erythropterus erythropterus,* consists of the interior of eastern Australia from northern Queensland to New South Wales. This bird has a length of 33 cm. The plumage is green; mantle and shoulders are black; wing coverts scarlet; the middle of the back blue; the primaries dark green; secondaries blackish; tail dark green, yellow-green at the tip; beak coral-red with a lighter tip; eyes orange-red to scarlet; feet blackish. The female is of a dull green; the outer, median, and greater wing coverts have red edges; the lateral tail feathers have reddish borders on the inner vane. In the Northern Territory, in the northern part of Western Australia, and in southern New Guinea live two smaller races, *Aprosmictus erythropterus coccineopterus* and *Aprosmictus erythropterus papua*. The Red-winged Parrot is charming, undemanding, and hardy, is not a screamer, and, except in the breeding season, it has shown itself to be peaceable in the birdroom and aviary. It has repeatedly been bred in captivity with good success. The incubation period is about 20 to 24 days. That the clutches are often infertile is due to the male's temperament. According to H. Hahn, this can be remedied by giving foods with a slight laxative effect, such as hemp, spray millet, and egg-food, in February and March. The Red-winged Parrot should be

accommodated in as spacious an aviary as possible.

In the closely related Timor Red-winged Parrot (*Aprosmictus jonquillaceus*), the wing coverts are only red anteriorly, otherwise greenish yellow. There are two races, one of which is found on Timor, the other on Wetar.

Red-winged Parrot. This species has a peaceful nature, except during the breeding season.

"*The Red-winged Parrot is charming, undemanding, and hardy, is not a screamer, and. . .has shown itself to be peaceable in the birdroom and aviary.*"

The Red-winged Parrot has become more available in recent years. It should be kept in a large outdoor aviary.

A pair of Salvadori's Fig Parrots. Fig Parrots are basically fruit eaters, but they often eat insects, lichen, and flower nectar.

Subfamily: taxonomic subdivision of a family based on some physical or evolutionary difference.

FAMILY MICROPSITTIDAE

This family, probably closely connected to the Lories, embraces 11 or, if one includes the genus *Psittacella*, 15 species of small parrots which are native to New Guinea, the Moluccas, the Solomon Islands, the Bismarck archipelago and the warmer regions of Australia. To bird fanciers they are only of minor importance since it is extremely rare for parrots of this family to be imported.

The Micropsittidae is split into two subfamilies, the Micropsittinae and the Psittaculirostrinae. If it turns out that the parrots of the genus *Psittacella* (four species, found in New Guinea), which at present are generally treated as members of

the Psittaculidae, also belong to this family, then these would have to be placed in a separate, third, subfamily (Psittacellinae).

Subfamily Micropsittinae All six species of this subfamily occur in New Guinea and on the neighboring islands, on the Moluccas, in the Bismarck archipelago, and on the Solomon Islands. They are the smallest of all the parrots (length 8.5 to 10 cm). In woodpecker fashion, they climb about on tree trunks and branches and feed on lichens, fungi, fruit, insects, and small seeds. Pygmy Parrots are imported only very exceptionally. The best known species is the Buff-faced Pygmy Parrot (*Micropsitta pusio*). This bird

Double-eyed Fig Parrot. Note the characteristic markings around the eye.

A group of
Lories at the
feeding trough.
Lories need a
special diet
and plenty of
room to remain
at their best.

A Double-eyed Fig Parrot. Note the prominent white eye-ring of this species.

Papillae: small protuberances on the surface of the tongue which aid in the ingestion of nectar and fruit pulp.

is yellowish brown on the forehead and sides of the head and blue from the center of the crown to the nape. The under tail coverts are yellow. The rest of the plumage is green. Length 8.5 cm. It occurs in northern and southeastern New Guinea, on the islands of the Louisiade archipelago, and on Fergusson Island as well as on the islands immediately off the coast of New Guinea. Within this range the species subdivides into four races.

Subfamily Psittaculirostrinae
The Fig Parrots are found in New Guinea, northeastern Australia and on the neighboring islands. Their diet consists mainly of fruit. These small parrots are little known, and imports can best be described as isolated incidents. The majority of these birds are magnificently colored, as is the Orange-bellied Fig Parrot (*Nannopsittacus gulielmiterti*), the seven or so races of which are distributed over New Guinea, Salawati, and the Aru Islands. In this species forehead and crown are

blue, blackish brown, black, or brown, depending on the race. The sides of the head have yellow or (again depending on race) blackish blue, white and yellow or orange markings. The breast is orange in the male, yellowish green in the female. The rest of the plumage is green. Length 13 cm.

The Double-eyed Fig Parrot (*Opopsitta diophthalma*) is red and blue on the head, yellow on the flanks, otherwise green. There are about eight races, distributed over New Guinea, the Aru Islands, and parts of the coastal region of eastern Australia. The female is distinguished from the male by having brown cheeks instead of red ones. The length is 14 cm.

The three species of the genus *Psittaculirostris* have extended feathers on the sides of the head, Salvadori's Fig Parrot (*Psittaculirostris salvadorii*) from northern New Guinea being one example. It measures 19 cm in length and, like the two other members of its genus, is thus larger than the Fig Parrots of the genera *Nannopsittacus* and *Opopsitta*. The male is blue-green on the forehead; there is a blue spot behind the eye; nape and extended feathers on the sides of the head are yellow, a broad band on the breast is orange-red; the remaining plumage is green. In the female, nape and sides of the head are green, the band on the breast is greenish blue. Fig Parrots feed on fruit, especially figs, but they also take berries, flower nectar, insects, perhaps fungi or lichens as well.

FAMILY LORIIDAE
This group is characterized by a narrow beak, an ungrooved upper mandible, and above all by the conspicuous brush-tipped tongue. This tongue, which is covered in fibrous papillae, enables the birds to feed on flower nectar, although they

also take tree juices and the soft contents of various types of fruit. Hence they are not seed eaters, even if some of them accept seeds of some kind or other from time to time. Lories are active and intelligent birds and very agile fliers. The coloration of their plumage is of exceptional beauty. Their natural range covers Australia, New Guinea and the neighboring islands, the Moluccas, the Lesser Sunda Islands (including Bali), Celebes, Mindanao in the Philippines, as well as numerous islands in the South Seas to as far as Polynesia.

The Lories form two subfamilies, the True Lories (Loriinae) and the Swift Parrots (Lathaminae), the former consisting of approximately 53 species, the latter merely of one.

A great many species have been imported and many of these have been successfully bred in captivity. The Lories do not deserve their reputation of being delicate and weak. This erroneous assumption can be traced back to the days when they were routinely fed on seeds, i.e., given a diet that was totally

unsuitable for them. If fed correctly, they do very well. But, as already said, they are not seed eaters, and in respect of nutrition they have been much sinned against in the past. In this conjunction I would like to refer the reader to an article on the diet of Lories by H. Lauer. Here is an excerpt from it: "I cannot agree with Dr. Russ's opinion that Lories can only be regarded as acclimatized and hardy when they have grown used to seeds as their staple diet. To me this seems erroneous since, as we shall see in a moment, it goes against nature and the method most closely adapted to natural conditions is invariably the best one. A doctor who had been living in Australia for some years and had shot and eaten many Lories told me he had never found seeds inside any of these animals. "There had been flower nectar (identifiable by the odor) running out of the beak, and insects, but no seeds. The long life span of Lories in captivity whose diet included few seeds or none at all also confirms this." He goes on to say: "For the keeper, of course, it is

A pair of Purple-naped Lories. This species may learn to speak and whistle.

"The Lories do not deserve their reputation of being delicate and weak. This erroneous assumption can be traced back to the days when they were routinely fed on seeds, i.e., given a diet that was totally unsuitable for them."

A Black-capped Lory. When first acquired, many Lories will scream until they become acclimatized.

A colorful Black-winged Parrot. Unfortunately, ornithologists know relatively little about the habits of this species.

A lovely Chattering Lory. The sexes in this particular species are identical in color.

much easier and far more convenient to substitute seeds for the natural diet. The latter causes considerably more trouble and requires the utmost care and attention since even the smallest mistake can have dire consequences. Soft food simply goes off too quickly. I always offered seeds to my brush-tongued birds in addition, but they never even looked at them."

According to a report by H. Hampe, the best food is the following: one tablespoon of instant baby food (in powder form) and two tablespoons of whole or condensed milk dissolved in a cup of hot water and generously sweetened with sugar, sweet fruit, and branches for gnawing. An alternative food is prepared by soaking stale, good quality wheat bread, pouring whole or condensed milk over it, and adding sugar. The mixture must be liquid enough to enable the birds to lap it with the brush-tipped tongue. At the Cologne Zoo, according to Chief Keeper Roelvinck, the Lories are fed almost exclusively on fruit, but it is important not to include too many bananas, as these tend to cause obesity. The birds also get a rather runny type of custard (made with corn flour, for instance) sweetened with sugar. The daily ration for a Lory is a full dish measuring 5 to 6 cm in diameter. A diet composed of the following is equally suitable: cooked rice, eggbread or rusk soaked in water, ant pupae, cooked and finely sliced carrots, and, above all, a variety of fruit such as juicy pears, oranges, figs, and bananas. In addition, they can be offered millet, hemp, and cooked maize, which are readily accepted by some species.

Considering their diet, it is not surprising that the Lories badly foul their accommodation. The smell alone is sufficient reason for a thorough clean-up at frequent intervals. It is advisable to equip the cage with a grid so that they do not get themselves dirty. In view of the active nature of these birds, the cage should be no smaller than 100 by 40 by 50 cm. Lories like bathing; they also like to spend the night inside nestboxes. They are hardy birds and perfectly able to survive the winter in a cold room or even in a sheltered outdoor aviary. The Lories get on badly with other birds and, in fact, constitute a danger to them. Noisy screaming is another fault of theirs, although they grow quieter in time.

Subfamily Loriinae In the six species of the genus *Lorius*, the Broad-tailed Lories, the tail is markedly rounded and little longer than half the length of the wings. The basic color of the plumage is red, but they have green wings,

often with yellow and blue markings. Many Broad-tailed Lories quickly grow quite tame. They also learn to mimic words rather well, with relatively little difficulty, and to whistle tunes.

The Purple-naped Lory (*Lorius domicellus*) comes from Ceram and Amboina (Moluccas); on the island of Buro it was introduced by man. In the past this was the Broad-tailed Lory that was imported most frequently and, therefore, the most popular one. It has a length of 30 cm. Generally speaking, it can be tamed quickly, gets onto the hand, and even allows itself to be stroked, which is something birds on the whole do not like very much. It learns to imitate words and to whistle tunes. When properly looked after, it proved a hardy pet and was not sensitive to lower temperatures.

The Black-capped Lory (*Lorius lory*) is imported from time to time. Its seven races are distributed over New Guinea, Batanta, Salawati, Biak, Misoöl, and Waigeo. It is identical in size to the Purple-naped Lory. Crown black; sides of the head, throat, lower back, rump,

Grid: a piece of wire mesh attached a few inches above and parallel to the floor which allows the droppings to fall to the ground, thereby preventing the birds from dirtying their feet.

A subspecies of the Rainbow Lory, Trichoglossus haematodus mitchelli. Some races of the Rainbow Lory have been successfully hybridized with other species.

A Red Lory in mid-flight. In the *Eos* species, the sexes are almost identical.

Mantle: the region encompassing the back, wings, and scapulars of a bird.

upper tail coverts red; breast and belly red down the sides, a band on the nape—sometimes a band across the mantle—of a lighter red; black with a tinge of violet from the back of the neck down to the breast and the mantle; center of abdomen, upper back, under tail coverts blue; wings green, more olive on the shoulders; under wing coverts red; lateral tail feathers dark red in the base, the median ones greenish; distal half blackish blue; beak red. What has been said about the preceding species more or less applies to this one as well. In its native range this beautiful Lory is a popular cage-bird.

The Chattering Lory (*Lorius garrulus*) from the Moluccas also has a length of 30 cm. The basic color of the plumage is a shining scarlet. The wings are olive green. The shoulders and usually a triangular patch on the back (the mantle) are yellow. Wings black; tail red, dark green at

the tip, with a tinge of violet. Beak orange red. The sexes are identical in color. This Lory again shows all the pleasant characteristics already described with regard to its two relatives. It would appear that attempts to breed this species in captivity did not succeed until a very late stage, since the first relevant report is that by N. Grasl. It refers to a pair of Chattering Lories, kept at the Schönbrunn Zoo, which produced one youngster in the summer of 1934. This bird lived at the zoo for several years. The pair bred inside an owl nestbox. The cage had the dimensions 2 by 1.6 by 0.7 m deep. The diet consisted of instant baby food, honey, assorted fruit, cooked maize, biscuits, boiled rice, and canary seed.

Representatives of the genus *Trichoglossus* have a wedge-shaped tail. The 12 narrow tail-feathers grow narrower still towards the tip. The two sexes are identical in color, but the females are a bit smaller as a rule and have a smaller head.

The Rainbow Lory (*Trichoglossus haematodus*), with its 21 races, is found from Bali and the Lesser Sunda Islands to Australia. Only the four best-known races shall be mentioned here, starting with the nominate form, *Trichoglossus haematodus haematodus*, which has a length of 28 cm. Forehead, cheeks blue; crown greenish; back of the head, ear coverts, and throat purplish black; a yellowish green band on the nape; breast scarlet, with broad blackish blue cross bands. Under wing coverts scarlet; abdomen green, yellowish towards the back, with green cross bands; flanks red, flight feathers green, tail feathers yellow at the inner vanes, beak red.

The best known race, since it is the one which is imported most frequently, is *Trichoglossus haematodus moluccanus*. It is native to eastern Australia, where it occurs from northern Queensland to Victoria and Tasmania. Its range also includes the southeastern corner of South Australia and the Kangaroo Island. It grows to a length of about 32 cm. It is easily tamed and can be trained as well. Furthermore, it learns to imitate words quite well and to whistle tunes. Unfortunately, it has a shrill and piercing voice. How peaceable it is varies, but under no circumstances can it be kept in association with other parrots of similar size. Being a good and quick flier, it needs spacious accommodation, like the other Lories. It has been successfully bred in captivity on many occasions. Crossbreeding attempts, with the Violet-necked and other Lories, have also been successful. The clutch consists of two eggs which are incubated for a period of 25 days. The young leave the nestbox at the age of about eight weeks and are then fed by the parents for a further three weeks or so.

Very similar to the above, but with orange instead of red areas in the plumage and with a broad orange band on the nape, is the race *Trichoglossus haematodus rubritorquis* from northern Australia.

The last of the Rainbow Lories to be mentioned here is the race *Trichoglossus haematodus capistratus*, which has a greenish yellow band on the nape, an orange-yellow breast, a dark green belly, and minium red under wing coverts. It is native to the island of Timor. Length 27.5 cm.

Another Lory with a wedge-shaped tail is the Ornate Lory (*Trichoglossus ornatus*), which occurs on Celebes and the neighboring islands. With a length of about 25 cm—the tail measuring a mere 7 to 8 cm—it is considerably smaller than the preceding species. Basic plumage color green; crown and ear coverts blue; cheeks red, behind them a broad yellow band; a red band above

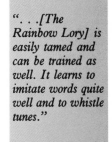

An Ornate Lory. This species is not as much of a screamer as are the other Lory species.

"...[The Rainbow Lory] is easily tamed and can be trained as well. It learns to imitate words quite well and to whistle tunes."

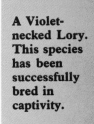

A Violet-necked Lory. This species has been successfully bred in captivity.

"The Scaly-breasted Lorikeet is a lively and charming pet, albeit not always peaceful and potentially dangerous to other birds."

"The majority of members of this subfamily [Platycercinae] rank among the most popular and most widely kept of all the parrots."

The Swift Parrot is the only member of its subfamily. It eats flower nectar and pollen like the Lories, yet it will also take seeds.

the back of the head; throat and breast adorned with narrow blackish blue cross bands; belly green in the center, flanks yellow; rump and under tail coverts yellowish green, wings black; tail feathers green, the outer ones of a dull orange color along the inner vane, red in the base; ceres gray, eye brown, eyelid bluish along the edge, feet gray. The Ornate Lory is a pleasant pet which screams less loudly than its larger relatives. It has been bred in captivity on many occasions. There have also been various successful attempts to cross the Ornate Lories with other species of Lories.

The last wedge-tailed Lory I would like to mention here is the Scaly-breasted Lorikeet (*Trichoglossus chlorolepidotus*). Its native range consists of eastern Australia, from the area around Cooktown in Queensland southward to central New South Wales. It grows to a length of 25 cm. Basic color green. Feathers of the underside and upper back with yellow parts at the root, hence the scale effect. Under wing coverts red, tail feathers yellow below, with

narrow red borders on the inner vane of the root. Flight feathers have a pale red spot in the middle of the inner vane. Beak red. The Scaly-breasted Lorikeet is a lively and charming pet, albeit not always peaceful and potentially dangerous to smaller birds. According to Neunzig, it was first bred in captivity in 1890, at the Berlin Zoo, i.e., inside a glass cage with an area of one square meter and a height of 1 m. The nestbox had a clear width of 25 cm and a height of 35 cm. The clutch was comprised of two eggs, the incubation period spanned 21 days, and the young left the nestbox at the approximate age of eight weeks.

The basic plumage color of the red Lories (genus *Eos*) is carmine, and they have blue, violet, and black markings. Hence they bear a slight resemblance to the Broad-tailed Lories, from which they are distinguished, however, by the longer, rounded tail. The beak is red. The only one of the six species to be mentioned here is the Violet-necked Lory (*Eos squamata*). Its four races are distributed over the Moluccas and islands in the vicinity of New Guinea. It has a length of 26 cm. The Violet-necked Lory has repeatedly been bred in captivity. It has also been successfully crossed with *Trichoglossus haematodus moluccanus*.

Subfamily Lathaminae This subfamily consists of a single genus, with one species which has been a constant problem to taxonomists, since it resembles both the Loriidae and the Platycercidae; some believe it belongs to the former while others regard it as a member of the latter.

The Swift Parrot (*Lathamus discolor*) breeds only in Tasmania and on islands of the Bass Strait. In the winter it migrates from there to the mainland of southeastern Australia northward to south Queensland.

The Swift Parrot is a long-tailed bird of an elegant build. Its plumage is mostly green, with a blue crown, yellow lores, red forehead and throat, a dark red patch on the shoulder, wings with a dark blue border, and a dusky red tail. Length 25 cm. Swift Parrots feed mainly on flower nectar and pollen but also consume fruit, insects, and seeds. In the aviary they should be given the same diet as other Lories. They seldom appear on the bird market but have aleady been bred in captivity.

FAMILY PLATYCERCIDAE

The 25 or so species which make up this family can be divided over two subfamilies, the Platycercinae and the Neopheminae. Both are immensely popular with bird fanciers and are widely propagated in captivity. With regard to most species, imports from their countries of origin have thus become superfluous. Some species nonetheless continue to fetch high prices. A few species are rare even in their native countries, and the fancier should exercise restraint where these are concerned, unless he is able to obtain animals that have been bred in captivity.

Subfamily Platycercinae The majority of members of this subfamily rank among the most popular and most widely kept of all the parrots. Many are exceptionally colorful. Their native range consists predominantly of the Australian region. Most species are found in the steppe or on tree-clad steppe terrain.

The sole species of the genus *Purpureicephalus* is the Red-capped Parrot (*Purpureicephalus spurius*), which is only seldom imported. It grows to 37 cm in length. The length of the tail is about 19.5 cm. Native range is southwestern Australia. Male plumage: carmine crown, sides of the head yellowish green; nape,

A beautifully colored Red-capped Parrot. This species is infrequently imported.

The Black-capped Lory is a popular cage bird in its native range.

A Mallee Ringneck Parrot. Parrots of the genus *Barnardius* grow tame but have a strong gnawing instinct.

Call note: the cry of a bird used to attract other members of its species, often uttered during courtship.

back, wings green; upper wing coverts greenish yellow, breast and abdomen violet; rump, under tail coverts, thighs scarlet; shoulders, edges of wings, outer vanes of the primaries and primary coverts dark blue; median tail feathers green, dark blue at the tips, lateral ones green at the base, a black cross band, then blue and white. Beak horn-colored, eyes dark brown, feet grayish brown. The female is smaller and the colors of her plumage are less pure. The call note is a sharp gurgling sound which is repeated at frequent intervals. Its diet is the same as that of the other Platycercinae.

For a time, the parrots of the genus *Barnardius* were assigned to the genus *Platycercus*. Now, however, they are once again regarded as forming the separate genus *Barnardius*, as in the past.

There are six races of the Mallee Ringneck Parrot (*Barnardius zonarius*), which some authors distribute over two species (*B. zonarius* and *B. barnardi*) of three races each. These parrots are native

to southern, western, and interior Australia. Plumage is green, the edges of the wings of a lighter green, likewise the under tail coverts; crown blackish brown or green, depending on the race; cheeks blue or blue-green; a few races having a red forehead; a yellow band on the nape; lower breast and abdomen yellow or green, depending on race; primaries and primary coverts dark brown, outer vanes blue; the two median tail feathers are green, bluish at the tip, the rest dark blue with a pale blue tip. Beak lead gray, eyes dark brown, feet blackish gray. This parrot grows confiding and tame. It has a strong gnawing instinct.

Space being limited, only two of the six species will be mentioned here. *Barnardius zonarius semitorquatus* has a black crown, a red band on the forehead, a yellowish green underside, with the abdomen bluish green in the center. Length 35 to 40 cm. Range is the coastal region of southwestern Australia. *Barnardius zonarius barnardi* is from southwestern Queensland, the interior of New South Wales, as well as parts of South Australia and Victoria. Measuring 35 to 36 cm in length, it is smaller than the preceding race. Green head, red band on the forehead, a brownish black band around the back of the head, a yellow band on the nape, underside green with a yellow or orange-colored patch on the belly.

Unfortunately, these beautiful parrots have virtually become unavailable in recent years. In the past they were at least imported in small numbers from time to time and were also bred in captivity. With regard to keeping and nutrition, they do not deviate from the rest of the group.

Now to the genus *Platycercus* (Rosellas, or Platycercidae in the strictest sense of the term). These psittacine birds are found partly in woodland, partly on steppe terrain. They have a dietary preference for the seeds of numerous grasses, and at times of shortages they are forced to migrate over large distances within their range in search of water or food. Accordingly, they are very nimble and fast fliers, although not moving clumsily on the ground either. Their climbing skills, on the other hand, are less good. In captivity they prove undemanding, hardy, and long-lived. Allotted sufficient space, they also breed readily and, on the whole, reliably. Their voice is less shrill and penetrating than that of parrots which belong to other genera but are of similar size. The ability to learn to talk is not well developed, although there are exceptions. The gnawing urge is not very strong.

In most cases the sexes are identical in color, but the colors of the females are dull, on the whole. The females also tend to be slightly smaller. The Rosellas are fed on millet, including spray millet, canary seed and oats, hemp in small quantities, sunflower seeds, corn on the cob, plenty of fruit, all types of greenstuff, and immature or germinated seeds. Where young are being raised, the following foods

Germinated seeds: seeds which are soaked in water, allowed to sprout, and are then fed to the birds.

The Ornate Lory has been successfully bred in captivity a number of times.

117

Ant pupae: intermediate metamorphic stage of members of the family Formicidae which comes after the larval stage and before sexual maturity.

need to be provided in addition: fresh ant pupae, hard-boiled egg, rusks, a commercial soft-food mix, and mealworms. Fresh branches for gnawing, especially from fruit trees, must not be forgotten. All Rosellas are fond of bathing. These lively and fast-flying parrots should be accommodated only in spacious cages. Aviaries would be better still, and it is only here that their beauty comes fully into its own. In a small cage the reverse is the case; here they are very quiet and downright boring.

They can be allowed to share more spacious accommodations with other kinds of birds, especially more agile ones, but not with members of their own species or birds of related species, as they are often quite cantankerous, if not positively malicious. This applies above all in the breeding season. At this time the pair must be allowed to have the accommodation to themselves. A special nestbox for large parrots (commercially available) should be provided. For the smaller species

Artist's rendering of three races of the Mallee Ringneck Parrot.

A Red Lory, Eos bornea. Members of the genus Eos are collectively called red Lories, although each species has a specific common name.

this should have a clear width of 25 to 30 cm and a clear height of 35 to 40 cm; for the larger ones the clear width should be between 40 and 60 cm, at a corresponding height. Depending on the size of the species, the entrance hole should be about 8 to 9 cm in diameter. Some animals prefer nestboxes made from natural tree trunks. A few *Platycercus* species (Crimson Rosellas, Eastern Rosellas, Western Rosellas, and Yellow Rosellas) can safely be allowed to spend the winter in outdoor aviaries with a temperate

shelter. The Pale-headed Rosella and the Northern Rosella, on the other hand, need a heated room for the winter months. The same applies to the small northern race of the Crimson Rosella. One additional point to note is that Rosellas have little difficulty in biting through the ordinary hexagonal wire netting that is often used.

A particularly interesting member of this genus is the Crimson Rosella (*Platycercus elegans*). The unusual characteristic of this species is that the color of its plumage can be

Entrance hole: the opening in the front of the nestbox through which birds go in and out.

119

anything from dark crimson to light yellow, depending on the geographical race and the climate that prevails within the latter's range of distribution. In the northernmost and smallest race, *Platycercus elegans nigrescens* from the coastal regions of northern Queensland, the head, underside, and the borders of the black feathers on the back are bright crimson; whereas the color of *Platycercus elegans elegans*, from the woodlands of southern Queensland, Victoria, and the southeastern parts of South Australia, is of a much lighter shade in the corresponding areas of the plumage. Where the latter is concerned, there can be considerable deviations both in body size and color intensity.

A third race consists of *Platycercus elegans adelaide*, which is a hybrid form and hence not surprisingly shows a great deal of variation where the color of the plumage is concerned. Even individual breeding pairs often consist of animals that are quite different in coloration. In this race the underside is considerably lighter than in *Platycercus elegans*. Often one sees individuals with feathers of pure yellow on the abdomen.

The Yellow Rosella (*Platycercus elegans flaveolus*) from the interior of southern New South Wales, the

Darling, Murrumbidgee, and Lachlan range, is pure yellow on the head as well as having a yellow underside and black feathers with yellow borders on the back. The only red in the plumage appears on the forehead.

Very similar to the Yellow Rosella, from which it is distinguished by the green borders of the black feathers on the back, is the Green Rosella (*Platycercus caledonicus*) from Tasmania and the islands in the Bass Strait. This species tolerates lower temperatures rather well. Until recently the Yellow Rosella was regarded by some scientists as a race of the Green Rosella.

The aviculturist who breeds Crimson Rosellas will be interested to hear that the immature plumage of *P. elegans nigrescens* and *P. elegans elegans* differs in that the young birds of the former have a red plumage when they leave the nest, whereas the immature plumage of the latter is green, and the red adult coloration is not assumed until the following year. Where red and green nestlings are being raised simultaneously, this can indicate that the parent birds are not purebred or that earlier generations bred in captivity were not purchased as purebred birds, i.e., that the two races, *P. e. nigrescens* and *P. e.*

The voice of the Pale-headed Rosella is louder than those of its close relations.

elegans, have been mixed.

However, as experiments have shown, it can also have an entirely different cause, namely the inadequate nutrition of young birds in the nest. This delays feather development, i.e., the feathers are not formed until the body has adjusted to the growth of red feathers as in the adult plumage, and the development of the green feathers of the normal juvenile plumage no longer takes place. A. Preussiger shares his experiences with young red and green Crimson Rosellas in that respect, and explains the results of the experiments from a scientific point of view. To the aviculturist he gives the following advice: "If you want to be sure of getting good birds for breeding, you need to buy animals which had a green plumage when they left the nest. With these you can be reasonably certain that they are in good condition, whereas with red juvenile birds one cannot always be."

Undoubtedly the best known species of the genus *Platycercus* is the

Eastern Rosella (*Platycercus eximius*), of which there are three races: the actual Eastern Rosella, *Platycercus eximius eximius,* length 30 to 32 cm, native to southern New South Wales, Victoria, and the southeastern parts of South Australia and introduced near Auckland and Dunedin in New Zealand; *Platycercus eximius ceciliae* from the interior of southern Queensland and New South Wales, differentiated from the preceding race by the pure golden yellow borders on the feathers of the back and by the blue (as opposed to pale green) rump; and, finally, *Platycercus eximius diemenensis* from Tasmania, which is more intensely colored on the head and breast than the nominate form and in which the red on the breast extends further in a downward direction. As far as I know, this race has not as yet been imported.

The Eastern Rosella is another species of which purebred animals have virtually ceased to exist, again due to excessive mixed breeding. This applies above all to *Platycercus eximius ceciliae.* Purebred birds of

Note the dramatic coloration of this Crimson Rosella.

"The Pale-headed Rosella has proven easy to breed in captivity. Its voice is louder than that of its relatives."

this race, i.e., with borders of pure yellow on the feathers of the back, are hardly ever seen now. Strictly speaking just a group of subspecies of the Eastern Rosella (since the two groups interbreed where their ranges adjoin), but generally treated as a species in its own right because of the major differences in the coloration of the plumage, is the Pale-headed Rosella (*Platycercus adscitus*), which, in turn, splits into two races. The nominate form, *Platycercus adscitus adscitus*, occurs in northern Queensland. It has a yellow rump and white patches on the cheeks, with a varying degree of blue edging. Eastern Queensland and northern New South Wales constitute the range of *Platycercus adscitus palliceps*. This race has a blue rump, and the patches on the cheeks are plain white as a rule.

According to Immelmann, in wild birds of these races the differential characteristics are not always clearly discernible, since the Pale-headed Rosella is characterized by considerable individual variation in

A pair of Pale-headed Rosellas. This species is considered by some to be a subspecies of the Eastern Rosella, due to the interbreeding at the boundaries of each species' range.

the coloration of the plumage, and sometimes the markings of one race even occur within the range of the other. In some localities one can find no two birds that look completely alike. The variability as regards coloration is further increased at the southern boundary of the range by the regular interbreeding between the Pale-headed Rosella and the Eastern Rosella; and the inevitable consequence is that many Pale-headed Rosellas have a greater or lesser proportion of Eastern Rosella blood. Here, where the range of one species overlaps that of the other, the immature birds are virtually impossible to distinguish. But not just here—right across the range of the Pale-headed Rosella, the juvenile birds often show hints of a red mask, although in most cases these disappear again at the adult stage. As suggested earlier, because of the extensive mixed breeding that goes on between the Pale-headed and the Eastern Rosella, it would be feasible to treat them as one species. The Pale-headed Rosella has proven easy to breed in captivity. Its voice is louder than that of its relatives.

Another red species is the Western Rosella or Stanley Parakeet (*Platycercus icterotis*) which, again, originates from southwestern Australia. With a length of about 25 cm it is one of the smaller Rosellas. Head and underside scarlet; a yellow patch on the cheeks; black feathers with red or green borders on the upper back, lower back green; wing coverts indigo blue, black shoulder patch; median tail feathers greenish blue, lateral ones light blue, white at the tip. Female smaller, the colors less pure. The two races of the Stanley Parakeet, i.e., the Western Stanley Parakeet (*Platycercus icterotis icterotis*), which occurs in the coastal regions of southwestern Australia, and the Eastern Stanley Parakeet (*Platycercus icterotis xanthogenys*), which lives further inland, show only minor differences in coloration. Thus the black feathers of the back and the wing coverts have green borders in the former while having red ones in the latter. Also, in the eastern race, the red underside is interspersed with yellow feathers. The Stanley Parakeet is not a screamer and gets on with birds of smaller species, too.

Another Rosella with magnificent colors is the Northern Rosella (*Platycercus venustus*), the two races of which are distributed over northern Australia. It looks very similar to the Pale-headed Rosella, except that the crown is completely black and the feathers of the rump and underside are pale yellow with narrow black borders; the under tail coverts are red. It grows to about 30 cm in length. The female is more grayish yellow and has a blackish brown head. This magnificent psittacine bird needs to be acclimatized carefully. Unfortunately it is only seldom available, all the more so since it is being threatened with extinction in its native range. Breeding it at least initially is not altogether easy, either, since it usually does not start breeding until October and its breeding cycle has to be adapted to temperate summer months first.

The genus *Psephotus* is comprised of five species, and its best-known representative is the Red-rumped Parrot (*Psephotus haematonotus*) from southeastern Australia (southwestern Queensland, the interior of New South Wales and Victoria, and the southeastern parts of South Australia). It grows to a length of 28 cm, the tail to 14 cm. The female is distinguished from the male by a greenish gray-yellow underside. The Red-rumped Parrot is a charming, lively, confiding pet. It also has a rather pleasing song and utters penetrating sounds reminiscent of a blackbird. Generally speaking, it gets on with smaller birds too—not,

however, with parrots of other species. In the breeding season it is aggressive, particularly during squabbles over nestboxes. It is hardy and long-lived and can be left in the sheltered outdoor aviary for the winter months. The Red-rumped Parrot is easy to breed. The nestbox should have a clear width of 25 cm, a clear height of 35 cm, and an entrance hole of about 8 cm in diameter. The clutch consists of four to five eggs, the incubation period is about 20 days, and the young leave the nest at the age of four to five weeks. Yellow animals have repeatedly been produced in captivity. In the periodical *The Foreigner*, E.T. Boosey writes about a yellow Red-rumped hen— presumably a wild bird—and a green male which together raised green young which, when mated among each other, produced one to three yellow animals per brood. The diet of the Red-rumped Parrot is the same as that of the other members of the group.

Another representative of the genus is the Mulga Parrot (*Psephotus*

A lovely Western Rosella. This species is amenable to other parrots and is not known for screeching.

"*The Red-rumped Parrot is a charming, lively, confiding pet. It also has a rather pleasing song and utters penetrating sounds reminiscent of a blackbird.*"

A male Red-rumped Parrot. Members of this species are lively, breed well, and have a pleasing song.

"...[The Paradise Parrot] may have become extinct. It was last observed with certainty in 1927."

The Mulga Parrot is a peaceful bird with a lovely song. It is, however, sensitive to cold weather.

varius), found in parts of west and inner Australia to as far as the interior of New South Wales, an appealing bird with a length of 27 cm. This species, too, is peaceable on the whole, with the proviso that also applies to the Red-rumped Parrot. Male plumage: green; forehead, band on the wing coverts, belly, rump, and under tail coverts yellow; a scarlet patch in the center of the abdomen, a red and blue patch on the upper tail coverts; primary coverts and edges of wings dark blue, the four median tail feathers dark blue with a black tip; beak of a light horn-color, feet blackish gray. The female is olive green-brown and has a red band on the wings. The Mulga Parrot has a melodious piping song. The diet is the same as that of the preceding species. The Mulga has repeatedly been bred in captivity. It is rather sensitive to cold and cannot be left in the outdoor aviary in the winter months.

In the past there were occasional imports of the Paradise Parrot (*Psephotus pulcherrimus*), which may have become extinct. It was last observed with certainty in 1927. Reports of subsequent sightings are less reliable. It is listed as a protected species, in accordance with the Washington agreement of 1975. Its range extended from central and southern Queensland to northern New South Wales. Length was 30 cm. Male plumage: crown, nape, back, wings brown; band on forehead, lesser wing coverts, abdomen, vent, under tail coverts scarlet; head, throat, breast bluish green; eye region yellow; rump, upper tail coverts blue; eyes dark brown; beak of a light horn-color, blackish at the base; feet yellowish brown. In the female all the colors are dull, the band on the forehead is yellowish green, and there is hardly any red in the plumage.

Like the Paradise Parrot, the Golden-shouldered Parrot (*Psephotus chrysopterygius*) is on the list of protected species. It is a small psittacine bird, measuring a mere 24 cm in length. Its two races are distributed over northern Australia.

In the males of the race *Psephotus chrysopterygius chrysopterygius* (range is northeastern Queensland) the plumage is as follows: yellow edging on forehead, yellow ring around the eye, black crown; upper back and shoulders brownish gray; abdomen light red in the center, under tail coverts light red; remaining plumage of head and body light blue; wings blackish brown with blue borders; median tail feathers olive green, blue towards the black tip. The female's colors are duller, the edging on the forehead is yellowish white, the throat and breast are yellowish green.

The second race of the Golden-shouldered Parrot is *Psephotus chrysopterygius dissimilis*, which is found in the Northern Territory of Australia from Darwin and Pine Creek to the McArthur River in the southeast. Black crown, dark brown

back, rump and underside greenish blue (the latter without red markings), under tail coverts salmon-colored, a broad golden yellow band on the wings. The female is mainly yellowish green, without any black on the head; cheeks and abdomen of a light greenish blue color. This parakeet is a great rarity. At the time of writing only very few pairs are in the possession of aviculturists. Breeding in captivity has often been described as difficult, due to the poor adaptation of these animals to the temperate seasonal cycle—in these regions they molt in the spring and get ready for breeding in the fall. It is essential that they be accommodated in a heated room during the winter months. Generally speaking, this bird has shown itself to be a reliable breeder. The first successful breeding attempt in

The Crimson Rosella shows great divergence in both size and color. Plumage varies among individuals from dark red to pale yellow.

Molt: the shedding of old feathers so that new ones can grow in, usually taking place before the breeding season.

Australian export embargo: a restriction that was placed on the capture and sale of all native Australian birds for the purpose of preservation of species.

captivity was reported in 1930. Hybrids of this race have been produced with the Golden-shouldered Parrot, the Mulga Parrot, the Paradise Parrot, and the Red-rumped Parrot.

Another member of the genus *Psephotus* is the Blue Bonnet (*Psephotus haematogaster*) from Australia. One of its four races is *Psephotus haematogaster haematogaster*. Upper parts, head, throat, and breast olive gray-brown; face, shoulders, edges of wings, outer wing coverts blue; inner wing coverts olive green-yellow; underside pale yellow, a red patch on the belly, undertail coverts yellow. In the

female the colors are less bright, the red on the abdomen is less extensive. The race has a length of 29.5 cm. It, too, ranks among the rarities, and this has been the case particularly since the Australian export embargo was imposed on all birds, but even in the past imports were few and far between. Another race of the Blue Bonnet is *Psephotus haematogaster haematorrhous,* from southern Queensland and eastern New South Wales. In this bird the undertail coverts are red and the smaller inner wing coverts maroon in color.

It is interesting to note that, in their natural habitat, some of the *Psephotus* species like to breed in the

The Northern Rosella requires careful acclimatization with regard to housing and temperature.

Kingfisher: a nonpasserine bird of the family Alcedinidae that is usually bright-colored, crested, and short-tailed with a long, sharp bill.

A pair of Golden-shouldered Parrots.

nests of termites, i.e., inside the deserted breeding hollows that kingfishers once built there for themselves. The deserted breeding hollows of bee eaters on river banks are popular nesting sites, too. As a last resort, when other breeding hollows are not available, hollow tree trunks are used as well.

Two of the strangest members of the whole group belong to the genus *Cyanoramphus*. These were more frequently imported in the past but now get to us only very exceptionally. The Red-fronted Parakeet (*Cyanoramphus novaezelandiae*) is protected worldwide under the Washington agreement. Thanks to this species being comparatively easy to breed, aviculturists have been able to

A Golden-shouldered Parrot and a Hooded Parrot. Like many members of the parrot family, the Golden-shouldered Parrot is on the list of endangered species.

"...[Yellow-fronted and Red-fronted Parakeets] are charming, active, fairly hardy, peaceable birds and have already been bred in captivity on a number of occasions."

Elegant Parrot fanciers especially enjoy this bird's song, which is said to be very pleasant.

preserve a limited stock. It is a green bird, more yellowish green below, with a red forehead and red crown; the wings have blue edges. The species is native to New Zealand and the small islands in the neighborhood. The Yellow-fronted Parakeet (*Cyanoramphus auriceps*), also from New Zealand, is similar to the Red-fronted Parakeet but has red only on the forehead; the crown is golden yellow. With a length of 21 to 24 cm, it is slightly smaller than the Red-fronted (27 cm). Both species are charming, active, fairly hardy, peaceable birds and have already been bred in captivity on a number of occasions.

Subfamily Neophiminae
Parakeets are small psittacines with a total length of 22 to 23 cm, with long tails which have a length of 10 to 12 cm. The four to six median tail feathers are almost identical in length, while the three outer pairs of feathers get progressively shorter. All seven species—which are distributed over the two genera

Neophema (six species) and Neopsephotus (one species)—are confined to the southern half of Australia, from central Western Australia to southern Queensland and the southeast. Although good fliers which often climb to great heights when covering longer distances, they do not make too much use of this ability but spend most of their time on the ground, where they run around nimbly and briskly. They are agile climbers, too, even among the densest branches. Freshly trapped wild Grass Parakeets are often rather delicate and, therefore, need to be carefully acclimatized. Once acclimatization has been accomplished, they often turn out to be fairly hardy and long-lived animals and are generally good breeders as well. Two species, the Splendid Parakeet and the Orange-bellied Parrot, enjoy worldwide protection under the Washington agreement, so imports are no longer allowed.

In a hobbyist's magazine, I recently came across the advice of an aviculturist who said it was perfectly all right to mate one male of the Neophema species with several females. This is a fundamental error, since just like most other parrots, the Neophema species are inclined to lead monogamous lives.

And now to the different species. The Elegant Parrot (Neophema elegans) is distributed over the extreme west of Victoria and New South Wales, a large part of South Australia, and the southern part of Western Australia. It has a length of 23 cm, the tail measures about 11 cm. The plumage is olive green, yellowish below, with a bright yellow patch on the abdomen. Stripe on forehead and eye stripe blue, light blue towards the back; lores yellowish, outer wing coverts blue, wings blackish blue, in some cases with whitish borders; the four central tail feathers grayish blue, the others yellow, blue at the base. In the female, the stripe on the forehead is narrower and the patch on the belly less brightly colored. The Elegant Parrot utters a rather pleasing song. It has repeatedly been bred with good results in the last few years.

A Red-fronted Parakeet.

"The Elegant Parrot utters a rather pleasing song. It has repeatedly been bred with good results in the last few years."

A Yellow-fronted Parakeet, a species which is easy to breed.

Imports of the Rock Parrot (*Neophema petrophila*) were a rare occurrence even in the past. The range of this species covers the southwestern and southern coast of Australia. Very similar in appearance to the preceding species but darker in color, this psittacine differs completely from the other Grass Parakeets where its habits are concerned. It is a pronounced seashore dweller, living and breeding among the overgrown dunes and cliffs.

The Turquoise Parrot (*Neophema pulchella*) occurs locally in New South Wales and northwestern Victoria. With an approximate length of 20 cm, it is roughly of the same size as the Rock Parrot. This magnificent psittacine, with an olive green basic color, a deep yellow underside, a light blue face and lesser wing coverts of the same color (the greater wing coverts are dark blue and there is a maroon patch on the shoulders), was considered extinct at one time but reappeared

here and there in the late 1920s and now enjoys a wide distribution again, although as yet only occurring sporadically. It is not of a particularly peaceable disposition. In the past this species was bred in captivity with good results. The song of the Turquoise Parrot consists of a rather melodious piping and twittering, but birds on the wing utter a loud two-syllable call note. Freshly imported Turquoise Parrots need to be acclimatized very carefully.

Undoubtedly the most beautiful of the Grass Parakeets is the Splendid or Scarlet-chested Parakeet (*Neophema splendida*),which is now rare even in its natural range. The latter extends from western New South Wales over the northern parts of South Australia to the interior of southwestern Australia. The species has a length of 20 cm. Upper parts green, face and ear coverts blue, throat and upper breast scarlet, underside bright yellow, wing

coverts light blue. The bird makes no special demands with regard to keeping and care. Breeding in captivity has repeatedly been successful and presents no problem, provided the birds are accommodated in a spacious aviary (this proviso applies to all the other species as well).

The Blue-winged Grass Parakeet (*Neophema chrysostoma*) is native to southeastern Australia and Tasmania. It has a length of 20 cm. Plumage: olive green; belly sulfur yellow; stripe on forehead, wing coverts, under wing coverts dark blue; lores bright yellow; cheeks and eye stripe yellow; wings dark brown, blue on the outside, with a narrow white border; the four central tail

A male Elegant Parrot. Like other Grass Parakeets, this species may be rather delicate when first imported.

"Undoubtedly the most beautiful of the Grass Parakeets is the Splendid . . . Parakeet . . . The bird makes no special demands with regard to keeping and care."

A Rock Parrot. This species lives in overgrown dunes and cliffs by the seashore.

A pair of Turquoise Parrots. This species was once in grave danger of extinction, but it now enjoys a good distribution.

"Already a rarity on the bird market in past years, the Orange-bellied Parrot has now ceased to be available altogether."

feathers greenish blue, the rest yellow along the distal half, at the base black on the inside, blue on the outside. The Blue-winged Grass Parakeet has repeatedly been bred in captivity.

The last species of the genus consists of the rare Orange-bellied Parrot (*Neophema chrysogaster*), which occurs in the coastal region of western Victoria and the southeastern parts of South Australia as well as in Tasmania. It grows to 20 cm in length. Already a rarity on the bird market in past years, the Orange-bellied Parrot has now ceased to be available altogether. The reason for this is not only the export embargo that has been

imposed on all species of this genus but also the fact that the numbers of wild birds have decreased drastically. Plumage: green; forehead, shoulders, edges of wings, greater primary coverts blue; throat olive green, underside yellow, a reddish yellow patch on the abdomen; the central tail feathers green, bluish at the tip, the rest yellow, black at the root, blue on the outside. In the female all the colors are dull.

The sole species of the genus *Neopsephotus* is Bourke's Parakeet (*Neopsephotus bourkii*) from Western Australia, the interior of South Australia, and from western New South Wales. It measures a bare 20

cm in length. The coloration of this pretty little parakeet is totally different from that of the *Neophema* species, since the former does not have a single green feather in its plumage. Rather, the upper parts are pale brown; eye stripe, forehead, outer tail coverts are pale blue; a narrow stripe on the forehead, a line below the eye stripe, and a spot under the eye are white, as are the cheeks anteriorly, the rest of the cheek being pale pink with brown feather borders; underside of a pale rose color (hence the alternative name Pink-bellied Parakeet). Rump and under tail coverts light blue; shoulders and edges of wings, greater primary coverts and under tail coverts indigo blue; wings blackish brown, outer vanes bluish. In the female all the colors are paler and the blue stripe on the forehead either looks faded or is completely absent. Bourke's Parakeet is an extremely attractive bird and a pleasant pet as well; it is undemanding, peaceble (towards smaller birds, too, which even includes waxbills), and not too

sensitive to cold. It can be bred successfully both in the aviary and in the cage. The nestbox should have a clear width of 25 to 30 cm and an entrance hole measuring 6 to 7 cm in diameter. The clutch comprises three to seven eggs which are incubated for 17 to 18 days, and the young leave the box at about four weeks of age. Some time ago there was a report of an albino.

The male utters a rather pleasing piping and twittering song which is not loud and does not get on the nerves of even sensitive neighbors. Bourke's Parakeet is often described not only as being quiet but as positively giving a sleepy impression during the day and (according to Neunzig, too) as becoming particularly active at dusk. My own pair in the garden aviary, where they were kept in association with various waxbills, Diamond Doves, and Chinese Painted Quails, also showed this behavior. The birds did not show any real signs of life until sunset. Then they flew about a lot

The Blue-winged Grass Parakeet, a native of Australia, has been bred in captivity.

Albino: a mutation in which both melanin and carotenoid pigments are missing, resulting in a white bird with pink eyes.

A Splendid Parakeet. This species needs a spacious aviary.

The Turquoise Parrot can be quarrelsome, and it needs to be carefully acclimatized to new surroundings.

and called frequently, and they kept this up until long after the sun had gone down. Only after the onset of total darkness (all the other inmates of the aviary had long since gone to their roosting places) did the Bourke's Parakeets finally settle down. To that extent it would, therefore, not seem wholly unsuitable to describe Bourke's Parakeet as a "crepuscular bird," although (as Immelmann points out) Bourke's Parkaeet is not crepuscular in the strict sense of the word; that is, unlike the Nightjar, for instance, it is not a species which engages in all the essential activities of its life cycle (such as feeding and drinking, mating, raising of young, etc.) at dusk. According to K.H. Bebensee, Bourke's Parakeet does, however, visit the watering places after sunset or before sunrise.

The diet of Bourke's Parakeet is the same as that of the species described earlier. In other words, the staple food consists of various kinds

of millet (including spray millet), canary seed, grass seeds, small quantities of hemp and maw, and plenty of greenstuff (all kinds). Fruit should also be given and, occasionally, ant pupae, hard-boiled egg, eggbread or rusk.

FAMILY MELOPSITTACIDAE

This family, which consists of a single genus (*Melopsittacus*) with a single species, the Budgerigar everyone knows, forms the link between the psittacines (from which it distinctly differs in build, however) and the ground parrots (Pezoporidae) from Australia. The latter, in turn—a family comprised of two species and of no significance to the hobby of bird-keeping—would appear to lead to the family Strigopidae, with a single species which is native to New Zealand and threatened with extinction, the Kakapo (*Strigops habroptilus*).

The range of the Budgerigar (*Melopsittacus undulatus*) extends over most of Australia with the

Bourke's Parakeets have been known to become active during the twilight hours.

Crepuscular: becoming active in the twilight, as opposed to nocturnal and diurnal.

A pair of Red-rumped Parrots. These birds grow to be lively and confiding pets.

exception of the coastal regions of the north, east, southeast, and southwest. A more detailed discussion of this little parrot everyone knows and loves should not be necessary here since other volumes have been wholly devoted to it.

FAMILY NESTORIDAE

Imports of parrots belonging to this family have never been frequent, although these birds are said to be easy to trap and tame and are relatively easy to keep as well.

Few, if any, are in the care of fanciers. By and large, they are found mostly in zoological gardens. The main reason for mentioning them here is that they deserve special interest. Evolutionarily speaking, they are among the oldest representatives of the order of parrots. Externally, these jackdaw to raven-sized birds differ from other parrots by the dark coloration of their plumage and by the structure

of the powerful beak. The latter is conspicuously long, laterally compressed, and the tip of its upper part goes well beyond the end of the lower mandible. Their range is restricted to New Zealand, where they are found in the extensive woodlands in the interior of the country up to the tree-line of the high mountains. They are not only agile fliers and climbers but also move nimbly on the ground. As distinct from all the other parrots, they are omnivores. They feed not only on flower nectar and plant juices, berries, fruit, and roots, but also on meat and, if necessary, carrion. Occasionally, it has been said, they also attack individual sheep from a grazing herd, injuring them (usually fatally) with the long and sharp beak in order to get at the entrails.

In captivity these parrots are given the same sort of diet as Lories. In addition, they get not only carrots and potatoes but also raw and boiled meat, although some authorities advise against the latter. They are lively birds, which means they

A male normal grey Budgerigar.

Opposite: **Artist's rendering of an Orange-bellied Parrot. This rare species is protected by endangered species laws and by an export embargo.**

Omnivore: an animal (bird) that eats both plant matter and animal food, i.e., both herbivorous and carnivorous.

A trio of Budgerigar hens—lutino, normal green, and light blue.

A pair of Budgerigars, a cinnamon gray cock and a normal green hen.

"Six Keas reached the Berlin Zoo in 1936. I remember them as interesting, extraordinarily agile, and lively birds that were forever on the go."

should be accommodated only in spacious rooms.

The family is comprised of a single genus, that of the Keas (*Nestor*). Its members consist of two living species and one from the islands of Norfolk and Phillip (*Nestor productus*) which became extinct in the 19th century. It is possible, however, that the latter was merely a subspecies of the Kaka.

The Kaka (*Nestor meridionalis*) splits into two races, one of which occurs on the northern, the other on the southern island of New Zealand. The species grows to a length of about 47 cm. The basic color of its plumage is a dark olive green-brown, every individual feather has a dark border; crown whitish gray, sides of the head and neck brownish yellow; underside, rump, upper and under tail coverts, and band on nape blood red; tail feathers black towards the tip (like the feathers on the upper parts); beak dark blue-gray, feet blackish.

The Kea (*Nestor notabilis*) is more familiar since it appears on the market more often. It is native to the

A Kea. The sharp beaks of the Nestor birds enable them to feed on carrion as well as on nectar, berries, and plant juices.

southern island of New Zealand. Length is about 50 cm. Its tail is particularly elongated. The basic color of the plumage consists of a dark olive green, and every individual feather has a narrow brown line on the shaft and a brown margin. Rump and under wing coverts of a faded scarlet color, primaries black, blue-green on the outer vanes, the inner vanes having yellow bands. Tail olive green with a black band below the tip. Eye brown, upper mandible dark brown, lower mandible yellowish. Six Keas reached the Berlin Zoo in 1936. I remember them as interesting, extraordinarily agile, and lively birds that were forever on the go.

FAMILY CACATUIDAE

The Cockatoos (18 species) are distributed over Australia, New Guinea and the neighboring islands, and one species has extended this range to the Philippines. They split into two subfamilies: the subfamily of Cockatiels, which consists of a single species, and the subfamily of the True Cockatoos. All species are characterized by having a crest of some sort.

Subfamily Nymphicinae The sole genus of this subfamily, *Nymphicus*, is made up of a single species, the Cockatiel (*Nymphicus hollandicus*). Its range covers the whole of the Australian interior, although it is only in the northwest that it is encountered regularly in the coastal regions as well.

The long-tailed bird (total length about 30 to 33 cm, length of tail 14 to 16 cm) looks like a cross between a Cockatoo and a parakeet. It is widely kept, since it is very peaceable and breeds readily. Although its voice can generally be described as a pleasant piping, it also utters shrill, penetrating sounds. It is easy to tame (this

Headstudy of a pearl Cockatiel, one of several color varieties of this popular, readily available cage bird.

applies particularly to juvenile birds that have just become independent) and learns to speak a few individual words and to whistle tunes. In a sufficiently large room, it gets on well with small birds, usually with Budgerigars, too. Finally, it is very undemanding as to its diet; millet, canary seed, and oats (also in a germinated condition) are perfectly adequate. During the breeding season, a few sunflower seeds, small quantities of hemp, and ant pupae should be provided in addition. It is a hardy and long-lived bird and, like many Australian parrots, can be left in unheated accommodation in the winter. In a reasonably spacious cage, it will breed readily. The nestbox should have a clear width of 20 to 25 cm, a clear height of 25 to 30 cm, and an entrance hole measuring 8 cm in diameter. Although young birds attain sexual

maturity at eight to nine months, they should not be used for breeding until they are in their second year, by which time their plumage will show the adult coloration. The average clutch is comprised of four to six eggs, which the parents take turns incubating, the female sitting at night, the male during the day. The chicks hatch after about 18 days, and the young leave the nestbox at 4 to 5 weeks. Cockatiels which have been raised in captivity are very pleasant, charming, and gentle, they become very attached to humans and, like the true Cockatoos, allow themselves to be stroked and fondled. According to Fr. von Lucanus, the females (which, incidentally, can be identified by the paler coloration and the barred tail feathers) do not learn to talk. Several cockatiel color forms have evolved in captivity.

"Cockatiels that have been raised in captivity are very pleasant, charming, and gentle, they become very attached to humans, and. . .allow themselves to be stroked and fondled."

A pair of yellow lacewing Cockatiels. Cockatiels come in a variety of plumage colors and patterns.

A flock of Red-tailed Cockatoos in flight. In the wild, Cockatoos often reside in large groups.

Cockatoos with black plumage are larger than those with white plumage coloration.

Subfamily Cacatuinae The True Cockatoos are powerful parrots of medium to large size. They are characterized by a very strong bill, the lower mandible of which is broader than the upper. In the majority of Cockatoos, the basic color of the plumage is white, in Cockatoos of one genus it is black, and only a few species do not fall into either of these categories. A characteristic which all Cockatoos have in common is the crest. This varies in length and shape, depending on the species. Cockatoos occur naturally in Australia, Tasmania, on New Guinea, the Solomon Islands, the Lesser Sunda Islands, the Moluccas, the Philippines, and on Celebes. They live gregariously, as a rule, in expansive woodlands, and feed on fruit, seeds, nuts, and tubers, as well as on insects and their larvae and on worms.

Cockatoos are of a sweet and friendly disposition, and are intelligent as well. Some of them also

"Cockatoos are of a sweet and friendly disposition, and are intelligent as well. Some of them also have considerable ability when it comes to talking. . . ."

A mixed flock of Long-billed and Little Corellas sharing a tree in their native Australia.

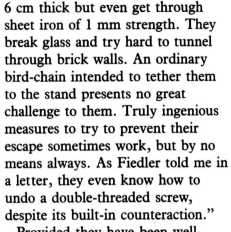

"Provided they have been well-trained, Cockatoos in captivity are exceedingly tame and affectionate birds that are a great source of entertainment and pleasure to their owner."

Opposite and below: Galah Cockatoos are known for their high intelligence.

have considerable ability when it comes to talking, and they have a special flair for learning all sorts of tricks, whereby their strong play drive and imitative instinct stand them in good stead. Their behavior can be extraordinarily comical; not without good reason have they been described as "feathered monkeys"! On the other hand, they gnaw terribly and are very destructive. "The destructive tendency is particularly marked in Cockatoos," writes Brehm, "and the achievements of these birds in that respect really defy the imagination. As I have experienced to my cost, they not only chew up wooden boards which may be as much as 5 to

6 cm thick but even get through sheet iron of 1 mm strength. They break glass and try hard to tunnel through brick walls. An ordinary bird-chain intended to tether them to the stand presents no great challenge to them. Truly ingenious measures to try to prevent their escape sometimes work, but by no means always. As Fiedler told me in a letter, they even know how to undo a double-threaded screw, despite its built-in counteraction."

Provided they have been well-trained, Cockatoos in captivity are exceedingly tame and affectionate birds that are a great source of entertainment and pleasure to their owner. Conversely, a badly trained Cockatoo is insufferable. Above all, with its loud screams it can drive its owner to distraction, and in an urban environment one would find oneself in an untenable situation. The keeper also needs to beware of the powerful beaks of these birds. A very strong metal cage is required! Truly tame animals, however, can also be kept on a stand.

Cockatoos are fed on maize, oats, sunflower seeds, nuts of all kinds, millet, canary seed, and hemp, as well as on fruit, berries, and carrots. Their strong gnawing urge necessitates the constant provision of fresh branches, and the gnawing also ensures that the beak is subjected to the necessary wear and tear. If fed correctly and treated well, Cockatoos can live to a fairly old age. A few species have been successfully bred in captivity.

The genus *Calyptorhynchus* contains birds of a black basic coloration, i.e., black Cockatoos. With one exception, these Cockatoos with very large and powerful beaks are native to Australia and Tasmania.

Black Cockatoos, considerably larger than their white relatives, are seen predominantly in zoological gardens, not only because imports of these birds tend to be rare but also

on account of their size. This applies particularly to the Red-tailed Cockatoo (*Calyptorhynchus magnificus*), which has a length of 65 cm, roughly one-third of which is taken up by the tail. The male is black, with a bright red band across the tail which is interrupted by the jet black color of the central tail feathers. The hen and juveniles differ noticeably from the adult male in that they have yellow patches on the head and wing coverts, there are orange-yellow squamations and bands on the underside, and the red band on the tail is interrupted by black horizontal bars.

The genus *Eolophus* consists of a single species, the Galah or Roseate Cockatoo (*Eolophus roseicapillus*), which is very common in its native range (Australia excepting Tasmania and most coastal regions). This Cockatoo (length about 36 cm) is a rather intelligent bird and is easily tamed as well. Over and above that, it can be trained to perform all sorts of clever tricks. Its ability to talk is nothing special, however. The Galah

has repeatedly been bred in captivity with good results.

The genus *Cacatua*, comprised of 11 species, splits into several subgenera, although some authors chose to treat the latter as genera in their own right. The subgeneric name is shown in parentheses behind the scientific name of the genus.

With a length of about 50 cm, the Salmon-crested Cockatoo *Cacatua (Cacatua) moluccensis*, is the largest of the white Cockatoos. It occurs naturally on the Moluccas, (i.e., on Ceram, Saparua, and Haruku), and it was introduced on Ambon. The white basic coloration is tinged with salmon pink, the bare eyering is of a light bluish gray, the wings and the tail are pale yellow below, the beak is black. In the female, the plumage is almost pure white.

An unspoiled Salmon-crested Cockatoo that has preferably been hand-reared from an early age probably makes one of the nicest, most amiable pets to have. Over and above that, it is regarded as the best "speaker" among the Cockatoos. A

A Salmon-crested Cockatoo. This species is the largest of the white Cockatoos, and as it has a large and powerful beak, it needs to have suitable branches upon which it can gnaw.

Some aviarists feel that the White Cockatoo has a plaintive and monotonous voice.

A White Cockatoo. This species is similar to the Salmon-crested Cockatoo, but it is not as lively, nor can it learn to speak as well.

bird like that does not utter those deafening screams either, or only extremely rarely. To my knowledge, there have been no successful breeding attempts as yet.

Very similar to the Salmon-crested Cockatoo, but with a length of 45 cm, is the White Cockatoo, *Cacatua (Cacatua) alba*, which has a crest of pure white. This species also has a black beak. On the underside of the wings and tail there is a tinge of yellow. The White Cockatoo is distributed over the northern and central Moluccas. Its personality is more or less like that of the preceding species, except that it is a little quieter and has a more monotonous, often plaintive, voice.

The Red-vented Cockatoo is not commonly available on the bird market. This bird is said to be quieter than most Cockatoo species.

When a generic name is followed by another in parenthesis, it means that some taxonomists use this name instead. Keep in mind that taxonomy is a constantly evolving science.

The Sulfur-crested Cockatoo is similar to the Lesser Sulfur-crested Cockatoo and makes just as good a pet; it is, however, quite a bit larger.

Its ability to talk is less remarkable, too.

The Lesser Sulfur-crested Cockatoo, *Cacatua (Eucacatua) sulphurea*, splits into six races which are distributed over Celebes and the Lesser Sunda Islands. It attains a length of about 35 cm. This species is one of the most frequently imported Cockatoos. Taming it is an amazingly easy and rapid process. It learns quickly and seldom bites. Its plumage is white, the pointed crest and the ear coverts are sulfur yellow, a bare eyering is light blue-gray to white-gray, the wings and tail feathers are yellow below, the beak is black.

Measuring 45 to 50 cm in length, the Sulfur-crested Cockatoo, *Cacatua (Eucacatua) galerita,* is considerably larger. This species splits into nine or so races which are distributed over Australia, Tasmania, New Guinea and the neighboring islands. The coloration of its plumage is identical to that of the Lesser Sulfur-crested Cockatoo, except that the bare eyering is whitish. This Cockatoo is an

extremely able pupil. It learns to imitate words rather well and can be taught all sorts of tricks. Neunzig describes a successful breeding attempt in an outdoor aviary measuring 2.5 m in length. The clutch consisted of two eggs which were incubated—alternately, by both parents—for about a month. The young left the nest at ten weeks of age, fully feathered but smaller than the adult birds. As breeding birds, the adults were very aggressive even towards the keeper.

An extremely talented and lovable Cockatoo with a small crest is the Little Corella, *Cacatua (Licmetis) sanguinea,* the two races of which are found in the interior and the north of Australia as well as in a small area of southern New Guinea. It grows to 40 cm in length. The basic color of its plumage is white, lores and forehead are light red, the feathers of the crest pale pink, likewise the roots of the feathers of the head and throat and (depending on race) those of the nape and abdomen as well. Flight and tail feathers are of a pale sulfur yellow along the inner vanes. In many cases this also applies to the ear region. The bare eyering is white to pale gray, the back gray to yellowish white.

The Little Corella is a good, distinct speaker. Despite initial shyness it quickly grows tame. Its screams are very different from those of the other Cockatoos; especially in the evenings one can hear its long drawn out, owl-like calls.

Goffin's Cockatoo, *Cacatua (Licmetis) goffini*, from the Tenimber Islands is distinguished from the Little Corella by its smaller size, white forehead and white lores, a bluish white eyering and the tinge of sulfur yellow on the underside of the feathers of the crest.

The Red-vented Cockatoo, *Cacatua (Licmetis) haematuropygia*, from the Philippines and Palawan, rarely appears on the bird market, and, when it does, only individual specimens are seen. It has a length of about 32 cm. Basic color white; a small, broad crest. The under tail coverts are light red. The feathers of the crest have a pale reddish tinge on the underside, the cheeks are of the same color, inner vane of flight and tail feathers yellowish, eyering white, beak gray-blue, yellowish at the tip, feet of a dark lead gray color. According to Neunzig, this species is quieter and gentler than its relatives.

The Long-billed Corella, *Cacatua (Licmetis) tenuirostris*, a white Cockatoo, was imported very frequently at one time. There are two races, one occurring in southwestern Australia, the other in the border region of South Australia, Victoria, and New South Wales. The nominate form measures about 40 cm in length. What distinguishes this species from all the other Cockatoos is its long, thin bill. The basic color of the plumage is white, forehead with red edging, red below the eye, orange-yellow above it, the feathers of the neck (visibly so anteriorly) and head are red at the base, and the bare eyering is blue-gray. The flight and tail feathers are tinged with pale yellow below. The

Long-billed Corella differs considerably from its relatives in its habits since it feeds primarily on the roots, tubers, and bulbs of a wide variety of plants which it digs up with the aid of its long and pointed upper mandible. Consequently, it also keeps to the ground more than do other Cockatoos. The Long-billed Corella grows tame and confiding, and it also learns to talk.

A Cockatoo of special beauty, if not the most beautiful of them all, is Major Mitchell's Cockatoo, *Cacatua (Lophochroa) leadbeateri*. There are two races, both occurring in Australia. The species measures 38 cm in length. Despite its less impetuous nature and its extremely powerful voice, this Cockatoo does not grow confiding and tame all that easily; it is an anxious bird. If the keeper succeeds in getting the bird to trust him, then Major Mitchell's Cockatoo becomes an extraordinarily amiable pet and learns to talk as well.

"The Long-billed Corella differs considerably from its relatives in its habits since it feeds primarily on the roots, tubers, and bulbs of a wide variety of plants which it digs up with the aid of its long and pointed upper mandible. Consequently, it keeps to the ground more than do other Cockatoos."

Salmon-crested Cockatoo showing off its lemon yellow wings.

Suggested Reading

The following books are recommended as supplemental reading materials. These titles, along with many others, are available at your local pet shop.

PARROTS OF THE WORLD
by Joseph M. Forshaw
ISBN 0-87666-959-3
TFH PS-753

Contents: This books covers every species and subspecies of parrot in the world, including those recently extinct. Information is presented on distribution, habitat, status, and general habits. Almost 500 species and subspecies are illustrated in full color.

The strikingly beautiful Major Mitchell's Cockatoo. This species is not easy to tame and requires patience and persistence on the owner's part.

Audience: This remarkable and beautiful book, valued almost as much for its sheer looks as for its highly valuable information, is a delight to bird lovers and book lovers alike.

THE COMPLETE BIRDS OF THE WORLD (ILLUSTRATED EDITION)
by Michael Walters
ISBN 0-87666-894-5
TFH H-1022

This book lists every bird species in the world and gives for each the family relationship, range, common and scientific name and related important data. Birds of 120 different families are shown in beautiful full-color photos; there are more than 550 full-color illustrations in total. This magnificent volume enables bird watchers, aviculturists, dealers, and scientists to learn the distribution, habitat, feeding and nesting habits, clutch size, incubation and fledgling period of every family of birds in existence. Written by one of the world's foremost bird authorities and illustrated with some of the finest natural history photographs ever published, this immensely colorful and useful book will be referred to for years regardless of where in the world the reader may live. This volume is fully indexed with both common and scientific names for easy reference. A treasure to own and a pleasure to show, it is one of the finest ornithological works ever produced.

BIRD DISEASES: AN INTRODUCTION TO THE STUDY OF BIRDS IN HEALTH AND DISEASE
by Drs. L. Arnall and I.F. Keymer
ISBN 0-87666-950-X
TFH H-964

This is a highly specialized book written for bird pathologists and dealers. Experienced bird lovers can recognize symptoms and diseases from the many illustrations and thus will be able to treat their own birds since "bird doctors" are so few and far between.

ENCYCLOPEDIA OF PARAKEETS
by Kurt Kotlar and Karl Heinz Spitzer
ISBN 0-86622-926-4
TFH H-1094

This book covers the long-tailed members of the parrot family generally in their housing, dietary, breeding, and health needs. The thorough coverage ranges from little known species like the Night Parakeet to the familiar Budgerigar and Cockatiel. Species accounts constitute the main portion of the text, with worldwide coverage: the Americas, Africa, Australia, and the islands of the Pacific.

PARROTS AND RELATED BIRDS
by Henry J. Bates and Robert L. Busenbark
ISBN 0-87666-967-4 New Edition
TFH H-912

This is the "bible" for parrot lovers. It has more color photographs and more information on parrots than any other single book on the subject.

One of the best selling books on our list. New editions are issued regularly, with new color photographs added with each edition. Written primarily for the owner of more than one parrot or parrot-like bird. A necessary reference work for libraries, pet shops, and airport officials who must identify imported birds.

THE COMPLETE CAGE AND AVIARY BIRD HANDBOOK
by David Alderton
ISBN 0-86622-113-1
TFH H-1087

Author David Alderton, well-known for his books and articles on avicultural subjects, examines the whole field of cage and aviary birds. Treating the species by family, he provides current up-to-date information on both the popular species and many of the less commonly seen birds as well. Full-color illustrations help the reader identify the species and varieties along with excellently detailed illustrations showing the design of aviaries and furnishings.

TAMING AND TRAINING PARROTS
by Dr. E. Mulawka
ISBN 0-87666-989-5
TFH H-1019

This book deals effectively with Dr. Mulawka's proven methods of successful parrot training. In this volume, which is heavily illustrated with both color and black and white photographs, the author imparts his techniques for cultivating the pet parrot's innate abilities to learn.

Index